Before You Vote
What You Need to Know

Before You Vote

Before You Vote
What You Need to Know

Including
The Declaration of Independence, The Constitution of the
United States of America and The Bill of Rights

By
Larry A. Maxwell
Author & Award Winning Journalist

Dedicated

to

Herbert *"Bert"* Maxwell

My Father

Pioneer with NBC News & Television

He Taught Me the Importance of Being Truthful.

Published by Challenge International

1130 Perry Rd., Afton, New York

599 Route 311, Patterson, New York

GoodInformation.US

Cover Design by Matthew Reid Maxwell

ISBN-13: 978-1537166735

IBN- 10: 1537166735

Table of Contents

Section   **Page**

Introduction 7

First Things First 11

The Importance of Voting 15

Understand Our Form of Government 17

Important Warnings 23

Carefully Examine Each Candidate 57

Understand the Role & Purpose of
The Three Branches of Government 67

Understand the Duties
of an Elected Office 72

Conclusion 74

Appendix 1: Declaration of Independence 75

Appendix 2: The Constitution 79

Appendix 3: The Bill of Rights 90

About the Author 92

Index 94

Before You Vote

Introduction

The purpose of this book is to show the reader the importance of voting and to provide you with information to help you choose the candidates who will best represent you.

In the United States of America, most communities have some kind of election every year. Many people run for a variety of positions. Those who are elected have an impact, sometimes in positive ways and sometimes negative ways, on their communities, and some have an impact on the nation.

Every four years, there is an election to determine the next President of the United States of America. Each presidential election also includes congressmen, and many state and local officials running for office.

Here is a very sad truth. In America, millions of people never vote. Though candidates win elections because they receive the most votes cast, most candidates never get the majority of eligible voters, because so many people, who could vote, never vote. Most candidates, especially in presidential elections, usually win with less than one third of the votes, of those eligible to vote. Yet the results of those elections have an effect on almost every single American.

In the 2012, American presidential election, Barack Hussein Obama won his second term with less than 28% of those eligible to vote. How is that possible? According to the *2013 Federal Election Commission Report*, in the 2012 Presidential Election, President Obama, the nominee of the Democratic Party, received 65,915,796 votes and won the election. His opponent, Mitt Romney, the Republican Party Nominee, received 60,933,500 votes and lost. Obama received 51.1% of the total votes cast, Romney received 47.2%. Third Party candidates took a total of 1.74% of the total votes cast. According to the *American Presidency Project*, only 54.87% of the people eligible to vote in 2012, cast a vote for a presidential candidate. That means more than 105 million people, who were eligible to vote, did not vote. That means President Obama was re-elected with votes from less than 28% of those eligible to vote.

The same thing happened in the 2004 Presidential election, when President George W. Bush ran for his second term. According to the *American Presidency Project*, in the 2004 Presidential election, President Bush was elected with 50.7% of the votes cast, which represented slightly less than 29% of eligible voters.

Both President Bush and President Obama were re-elected to their second terms with less than one third of all eligible voters. An overwhelming 71-72% of eligible voters, did not vote for them and yet they both won.

If only 5% more, of those eligible to vote in 2004 or 2012, turned out to vote, and voted for the candidate running against the current president, at that time, the other candidate would have been elected with as few as 33% of eligible voters.

Since 1828, not a single president in the United States has even been elected by a majority of those eligible to vote.

Another disturbing fact is, those figures do not account for voter fraud, which various studies show takes place every year. That means, if you remove the fraudulent votes, they both actually won with even a lower percentage.

A Pew survey in 2012, discovered one in eight voter registrations is either inaccurate, out of date, or duplicate.

Unscrupulous politicians utilize that, as well as low voter turnout to propagate voter fraud.

Voter fraud has been around a long time. Some biographers, of the noted poet Edgar Allen Poe, claim he died as a result of alcohol poisoning, contracted during the practice of *cooping*. *Cooping* was a term used for a form of electoral fraud, in the 19th Century. People were either drugged, or paid in alcohol, to vote for people who died, but whose names were still on the voter rolls. Or they voted, using the names of people on the rolls but who were known not to vote. On 3 October 1849, Poe was discovered delirious, outside of one of the polling places. He kept repeating the name, Reynolds, which made no sense to those who knew him.

One form of voter fraud, which was part of *Cooping,* is known as *Getting Out the Dead Vote.* It is a practice which continues today. I will never forget a conversation I had, a few years ago, with a representative of a major political party in New York State. He proudly told me, his job was to *Get Out the Dead Vote* every year. He said his party would have lost a number of elections were it not for the *Dead Vote*.

If more people, who are qualified to vote, would get out and vote, it could have a tremendous impact on every election. If only 10% of those eligible to vote, who did not vote in the last election, had turned out and voted, the results may have been completely different for many candidates.

There are many reasons people do not vote. Some do not see the importance of voting, so they do not vote. Others feel their vote will not make much of a difference, so they do not vote. There are some who do not know who to vote for, so they do not vote.

Hopefully this book will provide information to help more people see the importance of voting. This book also gives some serious warnings, and examples, about the dirty politics which plague both sides of many campaigns. I know some people will get upset because of the examples presented in this book, because this book shows some serious problems, which exist at times in both the major political parties. Hopefully you will get upset by what people have done, instead of getting upset with me for having presented the information.

Footnotes are not used in this book because much of the information, in this book is presenting inside firsthand accounts from the author's personal experience as a historian, from his experiences growing up in a media family, and from personally working in the media and from his forty-plus years of involvement in politics. Most of the facts in this book can easily be found in history books or in the public record. A number of specific sources are cited in the text of this book.

Three very important founding documents are included at the end of this book: *The Declaration of Independence*, *The Constitution of the United States of America* and *The Bill of Rights*. All three documents were provided by the National Archives, word for word, using the original spelling (which differs in a number of cases from modern rules of grammar).

Hopefully this book, will help more people become more informed voters, before they vote, so they can then go out and vote, making a difference.

First Things First

Before You Vote there is some preliminary information you must understand.

1.   Are You Registered to Vote?

Voting allows people to choose their elected officials and to determine how they will be governed. It has a direct impact on everyone, as elected officials determine the laws, which people must follow, and the taxes they must pay.

Anyone who is a citizen of the United States, and eighteen years of age on election day, may vote in any local, state or federal election. You may also vote in your local school elections, even if you do not have children in school. The only ones who cannot vote are those a court of law has determined to be mentally incompetent to vote; or felons, while incarcerated, on probation or on parole.

Though you may qualify to vote, you must first register to vote. Most states have a residency requirement of about 30 days before you can register to vote. You can call your local town office, or do an online search, to learn how to register to vote in your specific state.

To register to vote in New York State, where I live, you can register online or go to your County Board of Elections. In Connecticut, which is right next to my town in New York, you can go to your Local Town Clerk's office (Connecticut does not have County Government). In both Connecticut and New York, you can also register to vote at the State Department of Motor Vehicles.

In America, there are no fees to register to vote and there are no obligations once you register to vote. Even though you register to vote, you are never required to vote.

Once you are registered to vote, you do not have to register again. If you register to vote in time for an election, you can vote in that election, and in any other election, in a primary or in any special election. If for some reason, you do not vote for a few years, you should still be on the voting rolls and able to vote.

In some areas you may have to register separately to vote in a school election. Check with your local school for details. Remember, in many areas, your school taxes can be about half, or more, of your property taxes. You should vote for the school boards, which put together your school budget. And you should vote to approve or reject those budgets.

If you change your address, after you register to vote and live in the same area, you may only need to file a change of address. If you move to a different voting district you will need to register to vote for that address, even if it is in the same county or state.

When you register to vote, you may also choose if you want to become a member of a political party. There are not any fees or obligations to join a specific political party and you do not need permission from anyone to join.

Joining a party does not require you to vote for that party but it does allow you to vote in that party's primary, where they select candidates, to run against candidates from other parties. It also allows you to run as a candidate for that party. Some states do not require voters to belong to a specific party to vote in a primary but you must belong to some party to run for an office.

It is important to understand some states have a political party called *The Independent Party*. Some people, when they register to vote, decide they do not want to join any party but want to remain independent. They do not realize by checking the *Independent* box on the registration form they have joined the *Independent Party* by mistake.

In order to vote in an election, you must be registered to vote by a certain date, before the election. Do not wait until a few days before an election to register to vote, something may come up and you may miss registering to vote.

2.　No One Else Can Vote in Your Place.

No one else can legally vote for you and you may not vote on behalf of anyone else. To do either is a felony, which is punishable by law.

3.　Absentee Voting.

If there is any possibility you know you may be out of town, or unable to go to the voting place, on the day of an election, whether business or pleasure, and you want to vote, you may request an Absentee Ballot in advance and cast your vote.

Make sure you fill out your Absentee Ballot, seal it, and return it in time. It is better to send it in earlier than on the last date it is due.

The problem with absentee voting is, your vote may not be counted. A 2011 Study, presented by the Massachusetts Institute of Technology (MIT), put together by Professor Charles Stewart III, reported 21% of Absentee Votes in the 2008 election were not counted. That means 7,772,960 votes were not counted. That is the election where Democratic candidate Sen. Barack Hussein Obama defeated Republican candidate Sen. John McCain.

During the 2010 Congressional elections, when Barack Hussein Obama was President, a study conducted by the Military Voter Protection Project revealed only 4.5% of the 2 million Military Absentee Ballots were actually counted. That meant 1.9 million Military Absentee ballots were not counted.

If you are concerned about being one of the 21% of people whose absentee ballots may not be counted, as happened in the 2008 election, or if you are in the Military and are concerned your Absentee Ballot may end up being one of the 95.5% ballots, which do not get counted, you may want to make sure you deliver your Absentee Ballot by hand, before the election.

The Importance of Voting

Voting is a privilege, which allows people to choose their elected officials and determine how they will be governed. It has a direct impact on everyone, as elected officials determine the laws people must follow and the taxes they must pay.

Many people around the world do not have the right to vote. Voting is a both a right and a privilege, which many people, in countries like America, too often take for granted. More than 240 years ago, people in America fought a revolution, against an oppressive constitutional monarchy, which was over taxing them, without representation. They fought to get the right to vote and to determine how they would be taxed.

Many people do not realize, their vote can make a difference. The Town Supervisor in Patterson, New York, where I live, told me, that in Patterson, which has a population of about 11,000 people, anyone could win an election, if only 1,200 people voted for them, because of traditionally low voter turnout. He won his final primary with just three votes. I spoke with a family, which included three registered voters who voted for him. They proudly told me they all voted for that supervisor and that their three votes helped him win the primary. They were correct. That one family made a difference.

Can one vote change the outcome of an election? Just ask people in the State of Texas. On 27 February 1845, when Texas was a separate Republic, the United States Senate voted whether to admit Texas into the Union as a state. The vote in the Senate was a tie, with 26 *yes* votes to 26 *no* votes. Sen. Harry Johnson of Louisiana, changed his vote to *yes*. That one vote changed the outcome and Texas was invited to join the Union.

In 1839, Democrat candidate Marcus Morton won the Massachusetts governorship with 51,034 votes out of 102,066 votes cast. If he had received only one less vote, the election would have been sent to the opposing Whig controlled legislature, the party he opposed. and he surely would have lost. In 1840, Morton ran for re-election and lost. Then, in 1842, he ran again and won by only one vote in the state legislature.

In 1910, Democrat candidate Charles B. Smith ran for a congressional seat in Buffalo, New York. He won 20,685 votes and defeated incumbent Republican De Alva S. Alexander, by only one vote.

Your vote does make a difference. Get informed then exercise your right, and your privilege, and go cast your vote in every election. Your vote does make a difference and may end up deciding an election.

Understand Our Form of Government

Most people do not truly understand the form of government America follows. You do not need to take a course in political science, nor do you need to understand how other governments are organized, but it is good idea to understand what form of government the United States follows, so you can understand how it works and see how you can make a difference.

America is a *Democracy*. In most people's minds, a *Democracy* means the majority rules. Though America is a *Democracy*, there are cases in America, where it does not appear the majority rules. For example, four times in America's history, four men, who did not win the popular vote, became President of the United States. Those four men were: John Quincy Adams, Rutherford B. Hayes, Benjamin Harrison and George W. Bush. The reason that happened is because America is also a *Republic*.

Under a *Republican* form of government, the people elect representatives, who run the government for them, according to a *Rule of Law*. The *Rule of Law* in America is the United States Constitution.

The Constitution sets forth the procedure to elect a President. All registered voters may vote for the President but it is the vote of, what has come to be known as, the *Electoral College*, which casts the votes, which determine which candidate becomes president. The Constitution allocates the number of electoral votes each state receives. It is the total of each state's Senators and Members of the House of Representatives. That means some states have many more electoral votes, than other states. As this book goes to print, 48 states give the winner of the general election, in their state, all of their votes in the *Electoral College.* That winner-take-all policy is not in the Constitution. That policy was determined by each state, starting in 1828. A candidate may win the popular vote, yet lose the vote in the *Electoral College.* That is why it is important a candidate win as many states, with as many votes in the *Electoral College,* as possible.

In the 1960 election, Democrat John F. Kennedy barely won the popular vote with, 49.72 percent of the vote. His opponent, Republican Richard M. Nixon won 49.55 percent of the vote. Nixon won more states, taking 26 states, while Kennedy only won 23. Yet Kennedy won the *Electoral College* with a majority and became president because he won states with more electoral votes.

In 1984, Republican Ronald Reagan won 58 percent of the vote in the general election. He also won the majority of the votes in 49 states, so he won the election with more than 97% of the *Electoral College* votes.

On the other hand, in the 2000 election, Democrat Al Gore won the popular vote by a very small margin. He received 48.4 percent of the popular vote, Republican George W. Bush, received 47.9 percent. Yet George W. Bush won 30 states and Al Gore won only 20 states. George W. Bush won the election with 50.37% of the *Electoral College* votes.

It is important to understand America is not just a *Democracy* or a *Republic.* We are a *Democratic Republic.*

1.   What is a Democratic Republic?

A *Democracy* is a form of government where the power is held by the people, and the majority rules, either directly or indirectly, through elected representatives. There are a number of democracies around the world besides America, such as South Korea and India, the largest *Democracy* in the world.

A *Democracy* is contrasted with an *Oligarchy*. In a Democracy, the power is held by the people, in an *Oligarchy* the power is held by one individual: as in an absolute monarchy or a dictatorship; or the power is held by a few, such as in The Russian Federation and China.

A *Republic* is a form of government where the power rests with the people, but the government is run by elected representatives, who exercise power according to a *Rule of Law*. Rome was a *Republic* at one time. There are many Republics around the world. America is a *Republic*.

In America, the thing that distinguishes us from so many other nations, is our *Rule of Law*. The United States Constitution is our *Rule of Law*. Elected officials are elected to serve, at the will of the people and are to rule, guided by the United States Constitution.

2.   Are We a Christian Nation?

Is America a Christian Nation? For many years most people would have responded, yes, to that question. Times have changed and now there is hostility among a number of people against Christianity. So the question, *Is America a Christian Nation* is now a controversial question.

Opponents to the assertion that America is a *Christian Nation* often quote the *Treaty of Tripoli*, which President John Adams negotiated with the Muslim Barbary Pirates in 1797. The treaty was executed to protect American shipping interests in the Mediterranean. The Muslim Barbary Pirates declared they were at war with all Christian nations, like those they encountered in Europe, where most of the governments had their own official State Church. In order to secure an agreement with the Muslims, the treaty included the following words, *"The government of the United States is not, in any sense, founded on the Christian religion."* Those words were diplomatically chosen to deal with people who saw Christian nations as enemies. The treaty, which was basically a trade deal, did not say we were not a *Christian Nation*, that would have been untrue, instead it said we were not *founded on the Christian religion*. In one sense, those words were *technically* correct and helped America. The United States was not founded on the *Christian religion;* it was founded on *Christian principles*. The Constitution made it clear, the government should *not establish* any one *religion,* yet it must also *never interfere* with the exercise of religion. The Barbary Pirates broke that Treaty in 1801, when Thomas Jefferson was president. We ended up in a war with them. Our Marines fought valiantly all the way to the shores of Tripoli. The 1797 Treaty was replaced with another one in 1805, without any apologetical statements about Christianity.

On June 28, 1813, John Adams, wrote a letter to Thomas Jefferson and made it clear that the principles, which the Founding Fathers used to establish America were, *"the general principles of Christianity."*

Those *Christian principles* are clearly seen in the *Declaration of Independence*, which John Adams and Thomas Jefferson, both helped write and which the Founding Fathers signed in 1776. It became our first truly national founding document, as it declared our independence from the Crown. It includes these words, *"We hold these truths to be self-evident, that all men are created equal and are endowed by their Creator with certain inalienable rights... "*

The Founding Fathers acknowledged the *Christian principle* that all men were *created*, and that it was our *Creator* which gave us our rights. Those rights, given to us by our *Creator* are inalienable. That means government cannot give them to us nor can it take them away.

On September 3, 1783, the *Treaty of Paris*, officially ended the American War of Independence. That treaty included acknowledgement of the Christian God, yet not to any specific Christian *religion*. That official document included the words, *"In the name of the most holy and undivided Trinity. "*

In 1892, in the case of *The Church of the Holy Trinity vs. the United States*, The United States Supreme Court, gathered and reviewed thousands of documents written by the Founding Fathers of America. The court ruled unanimously that America, *"is a Christian Nation."* The court went on to explain that America being a *Christian Nation* did not mean that everyone in our country is a Christian, nor does it mean that Christianity is the religion of America, nor does it mean anyone is required to be a Christian. The court explained the fact that America is a *Christian Nation* because it was founded on *Christian principles*.

One of those great *Christian principles*, which America was founded on, was *Christian Charity*, also known as *Benevolence*. America has led the world with its *Benevolence* for more than 200 years, sending aid throughout the world, regardless of the form of government followed in the counties we were aiding. Many times, we even sent aid to those who have been our enemies.

We are a *Christian Nation*, because we were founded on *Christian principles*. Many of those *Christian principles* came from Judaism and we owe them a tremendous debt of gratitude. We must remember, our Constitution is clear, no religion is our official religion, no religion has a favored status over any other religion and religious freedom is guaranteed and should never be restricted at any level, be it local, state or national. Yet we must recognize that there are people, who have been seeking to eliminate any element of religion in our society for decades.

Our form of government is one of those things which helps make us an exceptional nation. We need to honor, protect and follow our Constitution, which is the basis of law to regulate our government. We need to make sure each branch of government stops overstepping the bounds set forth in the Constitution. We need to make sure we elect a President, who does not act like we are an *Oligarchy* overstepping their authority by virtually creating laws with executive orders. We need to elect a Senate and Congress which does not pass laws which restrict our religious liberties and freedom of speech, nor seek to impose government on areas of our lives, where it has no place. And we need to elect a President and Senate, which will appoint Supreme Court Justices, who stay true to the *Original Intent* of our Founding Fathers, unlike some of them who currently redefine the Constitution with their decisions and act like they are the ones who have the right to establish laws. If we do all of those things, then we can once again be a great nation and a bright light to the world.

Important Warnings

When our Founding Fathers established America as a new nation, conceived in liberty, it met with serious opposition. That opposition came from within and from without.

Many people are not aware opposition to our form of government, and to the principles America was founded on, continues today. Some opposition is subtle, some is blatant. It counts on an uninformed, uninvolved electorate. In order to maintain our liberty, you must understand the following warnings, before you vote.

1.   Sincerity is Not Enough.

Many people think sincerity is one of the most important qualifications in a candidate. I agree partially with that. Sincerity is a very important qualification, and one I look for in any candidate, but sincerity is not enough.

Years ago my pastor, Dr. Jerry Falwell, and I were discussing some people who had, what we felt were some very dangerous beliefs, which hurt other people. I mentioned how they were able to get others to follow them because they were sincere. He said, it is important to know a person can be genuinely sincere but be sincerely wrong.

Though sincerity is a very important, some people sincerely stand for some things which are not good at all. We must recognize that and oppose the bad things they promote.

We must also recognize that although a person can be sincere in a good way, about good things, they may lack other qualities necessary to be a good candidate. Sincerity is good, if it is about good things, but sincerity in itself is not enough.

2.   Do Not Trust the Media.

Too many people believe whatever they see, or hear, in the news. They think, *"It must be true, I saw it on the news,"* or, *"It must be true, I read it in the newspaper or online."*

All media claims to be unbiased but that is not true. They all have a very strong bias and do whatever they can to promote what they support and to cast those who oppose their bias, in a very bad light. One of the networks, Fox News, claims they are *"Fair and Balanced."* They may believe that, yet it is not true. They have a strong conservative bias, and do what they can to promote that position in the same way ABC, CBS, CNN, MSNBC. NBC and PBS, all have a strong liberal bias which they vigorously promote.

My father, Herbert *"Bert"* Maxwell, was one of the pioneers in television and broadcast news. After serving in the United States Navy, during World War II, he went to work for RCA, which owned a broadcasting company known as NBC. NBC radio had been around for a few years, but NBC television was new. Like many others at that time, my father worked for both NBC Radio and NBC Television.

He covered many presidential campaigns. He was there in 1948, when NBC presented the first televised presidential election night coverage. That was when Democrat Harry Truman surprisingly defeated Republican Thomas E. Dewey. The newspapers were so confident they knew what the outcome of the election would be, that they went to print before the results were final. They got the story wrong and reported Dewy won.

My father was there in 1952, when World War II hero, Gen. Dwight D. Eisenhower, ran as a Republican and became President of the United States. And then in 1960, when another World War II hero, fellow Navy man and Democrat, John F. Kennedy became America's first Catholic President.

He was covering the news on November 22, 1963, that awful day when President John F. Kennedy was assassinated. He was also working on the news June 6, 1968 when President Kennedy's younger brother, fellow Democrat Robert *"Bobby"* Kennedy also fell victim to hateful assassins.

My father was working on the news on February 20, 1962, when John Glenn became the first American to orbit the earth and then on July 20, 1969, when Neil Armstrong became the first man to walk on the moon.

As children, my father often took us to work with him. Sometimes he took us to NBC Studios at 30 Rockefeller Center in New York City, or to the Brooklyn Studios and also to various other events such as presidential primaries and inaugurations.

As a teenager, I was very interested in history and news. I remember going to the newsroom with my father and watching news come in from around the world on the teletype machines. I loved to read the news as it came in, line by line. Workers tore off the printouts and gave them to the writers or newsmen such as Chet Huntley and David Brinkley. The thing that surprised me was how many incredible stories they choose not to report to the public. It also surprised me to see and hear how the newsmen, added to, or omitted, details from the news stories I saw come across the teletype. I learned that day, you could not trust what was being broadcast and needed to question what was being presented on the news.

I will never forget April 4, 1968, the terrible day the Reverend Dr. Martin Luther King, Jr., civil rights activist and Baptist minister, was assassinated. My father called home from a news truck and asked us to pray for his safety. We could hear screaming and shouting and the sound of gun shots. He said he was in the middle of a huge riot. He said there were riots, looting and burning in many of the major cities. When we watched the news that night, they did not show any of the riots. Instead, all the networks said, the world silently mourned the passing of Dr. Martin Luther King, Jr. My father later told me the networks did that for fear the truth would have caused more riots. When I spoke with one of the reporters about that, he said it was not lying but manipulating the truth for the *greater good.* It was very enlightening to learn the media manipulates the news, when they think it accomplishes what they believe is the *greater good.*

There are two very serious problems with that attitude. First, it is alarming to know that the media, which most people trust, purposefully manipulates the news. The second problem is, that in their minds they are justified in manipulating the news because it is for the *greater good*, but who determines what is the *greater good?* That all depends on the bias of a reporter and ultimately on an editor. When the fascists and communists do that, they called it propaganda, but they are doing the same thing.

My father was bothered by the truth being compromised and twisted in the media. He instilled in me the importance of telling the truth, the whole truth and nothing but the truth. I never realized, after his passing, I would end up working in the media and have a chance to put his advice into practice.

My first job, working for the media, was when I lived in Schroon Lake, New York, in the Adirondack Mountains. I served as a reporter and photographer for *The Times of Ti,* a weekly newspaper based in Ticonderoga, N.Y. The editor from *The Glens Falls Post Star,* a daily newspaper, followed my writing and called me one day. He asked me to work for his newspaper as his Adirondack Correspondent. My duties were to go to events in the Adirondacks, and report on what happened, as well as take pictures to be published.

For each story I made it a point to report what happened, as well as why it happened. Some of the events I covered were community or sporting events. For those type of events, I attended the events, took pictures, interviewed participants and spectators and submitted the story and pictures to the newspaper. Those stories were often published, without any changes.

I also covered a lot of events, which had political ramifications. Around that time, the United Nations designated the Adirondacks in New York State as part of a special Biosphere Reserve. It was considered an area, which had to be protected from development and ruination by mankind. The United Nations plan called for removing large segments of the population from the area. The plan was supported by then Gov. Mario Cuomo of New York, the *Adirondack Mountain Club (ADK)* and other environmental groups such as the environmental activist group *Earth First!*

Gov. Cuomo had various state agencies pass regulations and take actions to implement some of the recommendations from the United Nations Biosphere proposal, without any legislative approval. Part of the plan included closing access to areas the plan designated as Wilderness Areas. That also involved removing structures in those areas, previously constructed by the state. Those structures included lean-tos, which were used by families and scouts to minimize damage while camping as well as removing fire towers, which were used for fire prevention. Those structures were called *visual pollution.*

Gov. Cuomo, had workers from the New York State Department of Environmental Conservation (DEC), place large boulders, to stop access into what the Biosphere Reserve re-designated as wilderness areas. A number of those roads were used, before his actions, to provide access to those areas by senior citizens and handicapped people, for decades. Local residents called those boulders, *the Stones of Shame.*

During that time, I interviewed one the members of the Board of Directors of the *Adirondack Mountain Club (ADK)* about the road closures. He said, he and his organization fully supported Gov. Cuomo's actions. He said, when he went for a hike in the Adirondacks he wanted to see things the way they were before man intruded. He said he did not want his view disturbed by people in walkers or wheelchairs.

Some of the members of *Earth First!* were emboldened by Gov. Cuomo's actions, and tore down the Fire Tower on Pharaoh Mountain, removing some of the *visual pollution.*

Unlike the *Adirondack Mountain Club (ADK)* and *Earth First!,* many people who lived in the Adirondacks protested Gov. Cuomo's actions. They held rallies, protests and motorcades. It became known as *The Adirondack Rebellion.* At one of those events, a group of senior citizens showed up with shotguns to stop state workers from blockading one of the roads, with more of *the Stones of Shame.* New York State Troopers arrived and the situation was tense. The workers finally backed down. I was told the only reason the workers backed down was because I was there taking pictures and covering the story. I discovered none of the guns, the protesters carried, were loaded.

I frequently spoke with Gov. Cuomo and his representatives, with leaders of *Earth First!* and with the leaders of *The Adirondack Rebellion.* I included statements from each side in every article so people could understand what was happening and so they could get the perspective from both sides.

My editor, Bob Bennett, had a very liberal bias and did not agree with the people behind *The Adirondack Rebellion.* He complimented me on my writing. He said he was glad I presented both sides of each story. He also told me he never received any calls from either side complaining about my coverage of events. He said, the sign of a good reporter was when both sides either hated or loved a story.

At one point, while I was writing for *The Glens Falls Post Star,* I went on a Missions trip to India, When I returned, my editor frantically called me. He said he wanted me to write a story they could publish, as soon as possible. He said, while I was away, he was flooded with calls from people who wanted to cancel their subscription because they did not see my articles in the paper. He said, they thought I had been fired.

Many of my stories in *The Glens Falls Post* were sent across the *Associated Press (AP).* As a result of that, my reporting caught the eye of the *United Press International (UPI).* They recruited me to be their Adirondack Correspondent. That meant every story I wrote had nationwide and world-wide distribution.

I received calls from people around the country who read my articles in other newspapers. I was flattered. I asked people to send me copies of my articles, which they read. To my dismay, I discovered some newspapers changed some of the words, or eliminated entire parts of the stories, I wrote, to skew the articles in favor of their own political bias. It reinforced again, what I already knew, you cannot trust the media.

There are numerous other examples I could give about how the media lies or misrepresents the news. On October 19, 1995, Louis Farrakhan, Sr., leader of the *Nation of Islam*, called upon African America men to join him for a *Million Man March* in Washington, D.C. It was a noble cause. In every news report the media called it *The Million Man March*. The media never reported the fact that Pete Piringer, spokesman for the *Washington D.C. Fire and Emergency Department*, reported there were only between 60,000 to 75,000 people present. It is amazing to get that many people together for a noble cause but that is 925,000 less in attendance than reported by the media.

On the other hand, the media greatly underreported the attendance at the *Restore Honor in America Rally* held on August 28, 2010, at the same location in Washington, D.C. It was hosted by Glenn L. Beck, television and radio personality. Some newspapers reported there were only about 10,000 people in attendance. I know many more people attended that rally, I was in there. When I arrived, two hours before the event, there were great throngs of people in front of me and behind me. I was told by the National Park Police, I was not allowed to go to the section where I was headed because there were already 150,000 people in that area, and it was closed. I asked about a second area and they said there was also 150,000 people in that area, and access to that area was already closed. They pointed me to another area where they said there I could go because there were only 100,000 people there, at that time. There were still thousands behind me and that flow continued and the attendance more than doubled over the next two hours. Shortly after the rally started, I spoke with one of the Police Officers in charge of the area around the Lincoln Memorial. He told me there were already more than one million people in attendance. He said he was amazed how peaceful and cooperative everyone was.

While there, I noticed political activist the Rev. Al Sharpton holding a counter-rally at the same time. I went over to hear him speak. He positioned himself next to one of the areas where there were thousands gathered for the Glenn Beck Rally. The media placed their cameras in such a way, to make it look like the people from the Glenn Beck Rally were there for Al Sharpton. I counted less than 40 people at his rally. I discovered, at least half of them were people from the Glenn Beck Rally, who, like myself, stopped to respectfully listen to Al Sharpton.

The drastic underreporting of the attendance figures at the Glenn Beck Rally and the placing of the cameras by the media at the Al Sharpton counter-rally, are another clear example of the way the media manipulates the news.

The media needs to be held accountable. Two websites: *FactCheck.org* and *Snopes.com*, claim they check facts and expose inaccuracies presented in the media. In some cases, they do a good job, however, you must be very careful using them because, just like the media, they have a bias. *FactCheck.org* is funded by the liberal Anneberg Foundation so a liberal bias is to be expected. *Snopes.com* is run by a husband and wife team, who claim they are unbiased.

Snopes.com selectively reviews stories and then corrects, what they see as inaccuracies. *Snopes.com* has exposed inaccuracies of some liberals, but seems to specialize in exposing the inaccuracies of conservatives. It is a sad truth, that too many times, conservatives use facts that are not really facts. Any inaccuracies should be exposed.

As I reviewed of some of *Snopes.com* fact-checking, I discovered they can be very selective in the way they present their *facts*. That was apparent when they omitted some important contextual information to support their claim America is not a *Christian Nation*, which was addressed earlier in this book. They also tried to debunk the claim that one vote makes a difference. They said it was false to claim that Texas became a state by one vote. They were correct in stating the vote for Texas statehood won by two votes, but they failed to present the fact that the original vote was a tie, and when one Senator changed his one vote, the invitation for Texas won. That selective presentation of the facts, used by *Snopes.com* is the same technique used by the mainstream media. Those actions lend some credence to those who criticize them as being a liberal blog.

Remember, never trust what you read in the news, or even of those who review the news. Be aware of bias. Be sure to carefully check things out.

3.   Most Politicians Will Lie to Get Elected.

One of the most disturbing realities to me is the fact that most politicians will try to tell you what they think you want to hear. That is a gentle way to state the fact that most politicians lie.

When I was living in the Binghamton, New York area I knew two people, who had two extremely opposite views on an issue. They both had the same congressman. I encouraged them to write to their congressman, tell him their concerns and see where he stood. He was a Republican. He replied to each of them. They each showed me his response. In his letters, he told each of them he agreed with their opinion and would represent them when the issue came up for a vote. That congressman wanted their vote and was willing to lie to try to keep their votes.

The fact that most politicians lie is not something new. Politicians have been lying for thousands of years. The disturbing thing is the way it seems to have become the norm for candidates to frequently and blatantly lie.

Many politicians refer to their lying as disinformation and justify it because they claim they are seeking to accomplish a noble cause. One example of that happened on September 11, 2012, when Muslim terrorists attacked the American Embassy in Benghazi, Libya. American Ambassador J. Christopher Stevens and three other Americans were brutally murdered. President Barack Hussein Obama and then Secretary of State Hillary Rodham Clinton said the attacks were in response to an anti-Muslim video. It was later proven both President Obama and Secretary Clinton knew the attacks were not connected to the video. They used disinformation (lies) to deflect the criticism of the way they handled the matter, which resulted in the deaths of four Americans.

I remember discussing the fact that most politicians lie, with a campaign worker for a Republican New York State Senator. That campaign worker told me his candidate was the exception to the rule. He lauded him as a beacon of honesty. Yet in the same conversation, he bragged about how his candidate fooled the public by painting Nazis swastikas on one his buildings, and then claiming his opponent did the task. He purposefully lied and manipulated the news. Less than two years later, a New York State commission revealed numerous improprieties conducted by that State Senator. The disgraced Senator had to cancel his re-election campaign and he fled the state.

4.   Watch Out for Political Correctness.

Political Correctness (PC) is a modern catch phrase, which affects a lot of things. Today, *Political Correctness (PC)* means using language or policies that are not offensive to specific groups of people, such as minorities, women, atheists, and the LGBT (Lesbian, Gay, Bi-Sexual and Transvestite) community.

The term was first used in the 1970's in debates between *The Communist Party* and *American Socialists*. It had a different meaning back them. It was used to claim the one group had a more politically correct interpretation of communism than the other. In the 1990's, the term was adopted and re-defined by the far-left. It entered the mainstream media in a series of articles in *The New York Times* and then was adopted as a standard in many of America's educational institutions.

It is always wrong to use offensive language against any person or group of people. The problem is, what is considered offensive language has been re-defined by the far-left to include any language, which any group of people they support, finds offensive. For example, when someone says the name of God, that is considered offensive to atheists, so that is considered *not Politically Correct*. Or, when a candidate speaks of abortion as the killing of unborn babies, that is considered hateful and *not Politically Correct*.

Though they will deny it, advocates of *Political Correctness (PC)*, either directly, or indirectly, try to limit the free speech of anyone who opposes them. If someone is considered to not be

Politically Correct, they label them as offensive and insensitive. That is a charge often leveled against conservatives by liberals.

One example of *Political Correctness* is the term *Native American,* now used by some, to refer to people who were previously called *American Indians.* Some White people decided the term *Indian* is offensive.

The term *Native American* was used for many years to refer to people born in America. One of the resolutions at the 1840 Ohio State Democratic Convention, criticized associations formed, which used the term *Native American,* because they were hostile to immigrants. Harry Houdini, the famous magician, was called a *Native American* in the March 7, 1915 edition of the Pittsburgh Post-Gazette. The article explained his parents were immigrants but he was *Native American.*

Russell Means, who was a spokesman for the *American Indian Movement,* said he and his people should be called *American Indians,* not *Native Americans.*

Some people have decided they will not have their free speech restricted by the *Politically Correct (PC)* crowd. As one enters the campus of *Liberty University* in Lynchburg, Virginia there is a sign which reads, *Politically Incorrect Since 1971.*

5.   Understand Big Brother Politics.

In 1949, English author George Orwell wrote a novel called, *Nineteen Eighty-Four (1984).* In his novel a strong centralized government, was run by elitists, for the good of the people. It was ruled by Big Brother. The slogan, which appeared almost everywhere was, *Big Brother is Watching You.* That government ran every area of people's lives. It was a cold cruel world.

We have many politicians in America who seem to think the idea of Big Brother is a good idea. They think most people are not smart enough to know what is best for them. They believe smart people, like them, should run the country for the good of those not as smart as them. They want a strong centralized government that regulates every area of our lives, including what we eat (telling our schools what they can and cannot serve our children), what we say (political correctness) and what we do or do not do (restricting our religious rights and other rights).

They want individuals to depend on the government and government programs, rather than the family or church, from birth to the grave, so people will be indebted to them and will have to re-elect them to continue those programs. They want the government, not the family or church, to be in charge of education, so they can control what is taught and make people believe their form of government is the best way. They believe government, not individuals should determine what health care they need. They believe government should determine what is right or wrong, not individuals and especially not the church.

Many politicians in office strongly believe in that model and are doing everything they can to help bring that to pass. That model is very similar to the platform of the Democratic Party. If you believe in that model you should vote to elect as many Democrats as possible. If you do not believe in that model, you should consider other candidates.

6.   Watch Out for Arrogance.

One of the things, which greatly disturbs me, and hopefully disturbs you, is when a person, and especially a politician is arrogant. I have little tolerance for arrogant people who feel they are smarter and better than others. Arrogance is pride in one of its worst forms. Arrogance often leads someone to say inappropriate things or take inappropriate actions.

In the 2016 presidential election, both the Democrats and Republicans choose arrogant people as their candidates. I cringed almost every time I heard either of them speak because their words were often filled with arrogant remarks. It is sadly not uncommon for some businessmen, like the Republican candidate Donald Trump, to be arrogant. It was very disappointing to see that arrogance from the Democrat candidate Hillary Clinton.

Though arrogant words are bad, the inappropriate actions that often accompany an arrogant attitude are even worse. Hillary Clinton's arrogant attitude has been manifested many times over her career. That arrogance became especially clear when she was appointed to serve as Secretary of State by President Barack Hussein Obama. With an arrogant disregard for the law, she set up a private e-mail server and discussed classified government information on that server. That is a breach of national security. If any other citizen did that, they would be in jail. One example of classified information discussed on her server, was mentioning Shahram Amiri, an Iranian scientist who provided intelligence to the United States. The government of Iran later executed Amiri. Some believe the fact Amiri was mentioned in emails on Clinton's private e-mail server led to his death. Whether or not that is correct, it was against all State Department protocol, and an arrogant violation of law, for classified information to be mentioned at all on a private email server connected to the then Secretary of State.

Another evidence of Hillary Clinton's arrogance was while she was Secretary of State. She sent her Chief of Staff to conduct job interviews for her private *Clinton Foundation*. Other government officials who lost their jobs for similar actions. Records also show many of the foreign dignitaries, she agreed to meet with as Secretary of State, made millions of dollars of contributions to her private *Clinton Foundation.*

The problem with arrogance is, arrogant people often do not think the law applies to them, or they believe the end justifies the means. That can make them dangerous people to have serve in an important elected position.

7.   Some Politicians Purposefully Hurt Others.

No matter how nice some candidates seem, many of them purposefully hurt others. I became personally aware of that back in 1972, when I was working on the presidential campaign for Democrat Senator Edmund S. Muskie, of Maine. Muskie was an exceptional candidate with high moral standards. It was alleged his opponent, Sen. George S. McGovern, of South Dakota, wiretapped Muskie and came up with some disparaging information about Muskie and his wife, Jane. McGovern's staff sent a letter to *The Manchester Union Leader*, the leading newspaper in New Hampshire, just two weeks before the New Hampshire presidential primary. The letter became known as *The Canuck Letter*. The next day the paper published an editorial attacking Jane, Muskie's wife. Muskie held a news conference where he broke down in tears defending his wife. McGovern's staff took advantage of that and said Muskie was too emotionally unstable to be president. Not long after that, Muskie withdrew from the race.

Staff members for President Richard M. Nixon became aware of the activities of the McGovern campaign. They then broke into the Democratic Campaign offices in the Watergate

Hotel. They were caught as they attempted to wiretap the office and steal documents. It is unclear whether President Nixon knew about the break in before it happened, but it became clear he tried to cover it up afterwards.

My fellow Muskie supporters and I were appalled to hear of the treachery McGovern committed against his fellow Democrat. The media however entirely ignored McGovern's activities and focused only on the activities of Nixon's staff. The Watergate Affair cost Nixon his presidency. The evil conducted by a Democratic Presidential Candidate lead to an evil response by a Republican President. It only proves how politicians on both sides try to purposefully hurt others.

The disgraced New York State Senator, I mention earlier, tried to hurt one of the two Sheriffs in his district, who would not endorse him. One of his staff members told me how he had one of his relatives call the Federal Bureau of Investigation (FBI) and tell them that Sheriff was involved in covering up a prostitution ring. The Senator then held a press conference saying that Sheriff was being investigated by the FBI. When reporters called the FBI, asking if the Sheriff was being investigated, they said they were not allowed to comment on a current investigation. That was enough to plant a seed of doubt in their mind about the Sheriff's integrity.

8.   Many Politicians Falsely Accuse Opponents.

Name calling and false accusations have been part of politics for hundreds of years. Politicians often call their opponent derogatory names. That seems to have gotten worse as the years have passed. It is not uncommon to hear candidates use such names as liar, racist, bigot, idiot, incompetent, woman-hater, liberal, conservative and many others, which evoke a negative emotional response by the crowd they are addressing. In many cases most of those claims are false, but they are effective because of the negative response they evoke in some people.

Politicians also make accusations they know are false because it makes their opponent sound cruel and uncaring. One of the most common false accusations is to say an opponent will take away jobs, benefits and health care from the needy. Those are very effective scare tactics.

When New York businessman Donald Trump announced he was seeking the Republican nomination for President, one of the things he said he would do was to evoke a ban, restricting Muslims from entering the country. President Barack Hussein Obama and Democrat Candidate Hillary Clinton immediately issued an outcry against him. They condemned him as a bigot for suggesting a specific group of people be banned from entering the country because of their religion. They and the media purposefully omitted the fact that what Trump said was in reaction to terrorist attacks, by Muslin refugees, which resulted in the deaths of many innocent citizens. They also downplayed the fact that the ban he recommended was temporary and conditional. They never mentioned the various immigration bans enacted by America against entire groups of people, both by Republican and Democrat administration. They also omitted the fact that President Obama and the State Department, under Hillary Clinton, had their own ban in place against a specific religious group. They refused to admit most Christian refugees seeking asylum from Muslim states. The administration went as far as to prosecute an attorney, representing Iraqi and Syrian Christian refugees requesting asylum. They contended Christians were not being persecuted, yet two million Christians were slaughtered in Syria.

The 2016 Presidential Campaign in America seems to have more name calling and false accusations that any other presidential campaign in American history. Republican Presidential Candidate Donald Trump and Democratic Presidential Candidate Hillary Clinton included intensely derogatory comments about their opponents in every speech.

When I was younger I was taught a saying, *"Sticks and stones may break my bones, but names will never hurt me."* The purpose behind that saying was to let you know you should not let it hurt you, if others called you names. The problem is, that saying is very wrong. Name calling can hurt much deeper than sticks and stones. I have a very hard time respecting anyone who calls other people derogatory names. I believe a politician should point out what they stand for and contrast that with what their opponent stands for but should never launch personal attacks. It is alright, and important, to point out any inaccuracies or lies and misrepresentations from an opposing candidate, but that can be done without name calling and personal attacks.

I like what Thumper the rabbit said in *Bambi*, the Disney movie. Thumper said, *"if you can't say something nice, don't say nothing at all."* The Apostle Paul said, *"Let no corrupt communication proceed out of your mouth, but that which is good to the use of edifying, that it may minister grace to the hearers."*

9.   Do Not Trust Political Ads.

Political ads appear on radio, television and in newspapers and magazines. Some ads come in the form of printed campaign literature. The purpose of political ads is to get a candidate elected. Some ads are paid for by the candidates, by their party or by other organizations. The problem with political ads is two-fold. First, many people believe whatever they see in print. Second, many candidates have no problem including lies, misinformation, false accusations and manipulated emotional appeals in their literature. Many candidates do not appear to have any problem lying. I have seen that in local, state and national elections.

Many candidates misrepresent information in their ads. For example, some candidates run ads saying things like, the rich have too many tax breaks and *Must Pay Their Fair Share*. What they fail to say is 10% of the population pay 70% of the income taxes collected in America and 45% of the population do not pay any income taxes at all. In fact, the top 1% of the population pays almost 50% of the income taxes collected in America. That certainly isn't fair. If they truly want people to *Pay Their Fair Share,* they would drastically lower the taxes on that top 10% who are paying 70% of the taxes and on the top 1% who are paying 50% of the taxes. If a candidate truly wants everyone to *Pay Their Fair Share*, they should support eliminating the Income Tax, where people are penalized for earning money, and institute a *Simple Flat Tax*, such as that proposed by Rand Paul or Ted Cruz. With a *Simple Flat Tax* people only pay tax on what they spend. People who spend more will pay more, people who spend less, pay less.

Do not believe what you see in Political Ads, from any candidate, no matter how emotionally compelling they appear.

10.   People Make Donations to Buy Influence.

It usually takes a lot of money to run a campaign. Politicians need people to make financial donations to help their campaign.

The problem is many people, and companies, make donations to candidates in order to get something favorable in return. That creates lots of problems.

It is interesting to see how many candidates speak out against certain issues but still take significant funds from people who are backing the very things the candidates *say* they are against.

In the 2016 Presidential election, Democrat Candidate Hillary Clinton said she was against big banks, yet received millions of dollars of speaking fees from big banks.

11.   Watch Out for Power Brokers.

There are many individuals and organizations who seek to influence politicians in many ways. There is nothing wrong with letting a candidate know where you stand and trying to get them to support legislation. The problem is when those individuals, or organizations, try to use their power, either financial or influence to sway or control a candidate.

There have always been power brokers, who use their power to influence candidates. Roger Ailes, who headed Fox News, was a very influential power broker for conservatives and billionaire George Soros was a very strong power broker for liberals. Mobsters were strong powerful power brokers in major cities like Chicago, Detroit and New York for many years.

Lobbyists are professionals whose job is to try to influence an elected official to sponsor legislation favorable to their constituents. There is nothing wrong with that. The problem is, some Lobbyist have multi-million dollar budgets they use to try to buy favors and influence, candidates and legislations. It is not unusual for them to become power brokers. Legislation to try to limit the influence of Lobbyists is often defeated.

Many Unions have been very effective power brokers with the financial support and votes they can deliver. Most candidates are envious for support from the Unions.

Individuals are limited as to how much they may individually donate to a specific candidate. *Political Action Committees (PACS)* are organizations, privately formed, which can raise money, privately, to help influence both elections and legislation. People can contribute more money to PACs, which have significant influence on candidates. PACS can often donate directly to a candidate's campaign, help raise funds for a candidate or spend hundreds of thousands of dollars on political ads, which favor one candidate over another.

It can tell you a lot about a candidate when you find out which Power Brokers, Lobbyists, Unions and PACS support them. Always seek to learn what other candidates those groups support, and ask yourself if you are comfortable with them.

12.   Power Corrupts.

One of my history professors taught us, *"All politicians are corrupt, but some are more corrupt than others."*

Over the years, I have come to know many politicians. From my experience, I would modify that professor's statement to read as follows, *"Most politicians get corrupted, but some get more corrupted than others."*

A number of people enter politics with good motives. They are sincere when they start. The problem is, they rub shoulders with people who have bad motives, and realize they need to raise finances or think they have to make alliances with unscrupulous people to pass certain legislation and they end up corrupted.

We often become like the people we associate with. Look at those close to a candidate. Look at the people who endorse them, and look at the people supporting them. Are those the people you are comfortable with?

13.   Be Aware of Voter Fraud.

Every citizen of the United States, age 18 or older is entitled to vote and should be encouraged to register to vote and be allowed to vote. Every vote is important. To falsely vote is a crime yet many people still do it.

Voter Fraud is a very serious problem because one of its main elements is casting votes, which should not be cast. That is why unscrupulous candidates turn a blind eye on voter fraud. The more votes they get, the better the chance they will be elected.

The phrase, *"Vote early and vote often,"* started to appear in American in the mid-19th century. Voting early is a good idea, but to vote often, implies casting more than one vote in the same election, which is dishonest and illegal. *Vote early and vote often* was a particularly popular slogan used in Chicago, during its notorious gangster era.

One of the best ways to stop voter fraud is to require each voter to produce some type of official photo identification, when they register to vote and when they come to vote.

Some people claim the requirement of photo identification, in order to vote, is discriminatory against the poor, women, minorities and ethnic groups. That is a false claim. There are many groups who gladly provide assistance for any person to get photo identification.

Everyone is required to provide photo identification for many things. In most states you need photo identification to prove you are old enough to buy alcohol or cigarettes. You need it to apply for welfare or food stamps. You need photo identification to open a bank account and you need it to pay by check in a store. You need photo identification to apply for most jobs and for unemployment. You need photo identification to enter a federal building. A person may not fly on a commercial airline in the United States without photo identification.

The Following are Some Common Types of Voter Fraud:

○ **Forging Signatures** – Forging signatures is a frequent problem with candidate petitions. A candidate for most offices has to secure the signatures of a certain number of names of registered voters, on a petition, in order to appear on a ballot for an election. We had a local candidate running for the New York State Assembly in our area in 2016. That person, previously worked for the former disgraced New York State Senator, mentioned earlier, who left the state after a commission exposed his corruption. That disgraced former State Senator helped run his former staff member's campaign. That candidate submitted petitions to the New York State Board of Elections to have their name added to the Conservative Party ballot. The Board of Elections determined the petitions contained 130 false signatures and removed their name from the ballot.

○ **Multiple Registrations** – Some people are registered to vote in more than one place. Some do it by mistake, some by oversight and some on purpose. It is voter fraud, to cast a vote, in the same election, in more than one place. When I first moved to Connecticut in 1972, I registered to vote. In 1976, I moved to New York, and registered to vote there. In 1979, I moved back to Connecticut and registered to vote in the same town where I previously registered back in 1972. When I went to vote in the next election, they asked me my name and address. When I gave them that information, they asked me, Which Larry A. Maxwell? They had two on the roles, at the same address. Both of them were me. I was still on the roles from 1972 and on the roll from my recent registration.

○ **Invalid Registrations** – Some people register with false names. In 2008, Mickey Mouse appeared on voter rolls in Florida. CNN reported that the *Association of Community Organizers for Reform Action (ACORN)*, submitted 5,000 voter registration forms in Chicago. The first 2,200 forms all turned out to be phony. Barack Hussein Obama had paid a subsidiary of ACORN $800,000 in that election to get the vote out for him.

○ **The Dead Vote** – A mentioned in the Introduction, people have illegally voted for dead people for many years. Voter rolls are available to the public. It is easy to compare the voter rolls with lists of people who died. In smaller communities the *Dead Votes* are often cast by Absentee Ballot, to avoid a personal encounter with a poll worker who may recognize the person voting is not the deceased person.

○ **Using Other People's Names** – There are people who review voting records, which are public information, to see who has not voted in the past few elections. They compile lists and have people get Absentee Ballots, or go to polling places in larger communities, and cast votes for their candidate, using those names. In 1979, when I discovered my name was listed twice at the polls in Connecticut, I was upset to learn someone had voted using my name in the last few elections.

○ **Nursing Home Votes** – Unscrupulous people go into Nursing Homes and other Assisted Living Facilities and cast votes on behalf of residents who are unaware or incapable to comprehend what has happened. In 1998, Austin Murphy, a Democrat congressman from Pennsylvania was convicted of voter fraud for going into a nursing home and getting people to put their mark on ballots for him, not realizing what they were doing. I know a man in one of the nursing homes in our area who asked his son to take him to vote. When they arrived at the polling place he discovered someone already voted, with an Absentee Ballot, using his name.

14.   Some People Get Hurt & Die.

This one may sound alarmist to some, but you need to know, politicians, and people who oppose certain politicians, or who pose a perceived threat to other politicians, sometimes end up hurt or dead. This has happened for thousands of years. Sometimes people are publicly assaulted or assassinated, while some die under mysterious circumstances.

When I was working as a reporter, covering the *Adirondack Rebellion* in upstate New York, one of the unintentional results of my reporting was, it put an end to the presidential ambitions of Mario Cuomo, then Governor of New York. I will never forget the day he pointed his finger in my face and said, *"Maxwell, I'm going to get you!"* I am glad to say that neither he, nor any of his associates followed through on that threat.

Sen. Charles Sumner of Massachusetts had someone get upset with him and hurt him. On May 22, 1856, Sen. Sumner, delivered a speech against slavery on floor of the United States Senate. Two days later, Preston Brooks, a Democrat, representing South Carolina in the House of Representatives, was so offended by Sumner's speech against slavery that he decided to punish Sumner with a public beating. He entered the Senate chamber, argued with Sumner and then began to beat Sumner over the head with his cane. He beat Sumner until he fell to the floor unconscious. Other Senators tried to rush to Sumner's aide, but fellow Democrat Laurence Keitt, held a pistol and threatened to kill anyone who tried to stop Brooks. Sumner lived, but it is believed he suffered a traumatic brain injury from the beating.

Others have been killed by their opponents. One day I had lunch with Gov. John Connally, former Democratic Governor of Texas. He told me details of how on November 22, 1963, He and his wife Nellie, were in a car in Dallas, Texas, with President John F. Kennedy and his wife Jacqueline. He said his life changed when he heard multiple gunshots. One of the bullets struck him and at least one of the other bullets mortally struck President Kennedy. That day, President Kennedy became the fourth United States President to be assassinated.

In 1989, I was scheduled to take a trip to India to speak in a conference and in various other meetings. One of the stops on my itinerary was a visit with Prime Minister Rajiv Gandhi. He had become Prime Minister of India after his mother Indira Gandhi, the first and only female Prime Minister of India, was assassinated. My plans were altered, before I left, when I received news that Rajiv Gandhi was assassinated. When I went to India, I stayed in his palace but was saddened that he was not there because he had been killed by his political opponents.

Another time, I was in the Philippines, with my good friend Dr. Benny Abante, Jr. He was pastor of a church and served on the Manila City Council at that time. He later became a congressman. We had lunch with President Fidel Ramos and then met with other government officials. Every place we went we were in vehicles with darkened windows, and took different routes. He said that was done as a precaution because his enemies wanted him dead. We heard gunshots on numerous occasions.

In America, people other than presidents have fallen to the assassin's bullets. There was Bobby Kennedy, brother of President John F. Kennedy, civil rights leader Dr. Martin Luther King, Jr. and Malcom X, leader of the Nation of Islam.

After the War Between the States, which is also called the Civil War, during the period called *Reconstruction*, a number of African-Americans, ran against Democrats and were elected as Republican Congressman and Senators. They ended up with death threats and bounties placed on their heads. A number of their supporters were brutally murdered by the Ku Klux Klan.

Over the years, many lives have been threatened and many have died because of their political involvement. Many, who were a perceived threat to powerful politicians have mysteriously died.

In July 2016, during the Democratic National Convention thousands of emails were released showing how Candidate Hillary Clinton and Democratic Party insiders worked together to stop her opponent Sen. Bernie Sanders of Vermont, from securing the Democratic Party Nomination for President. The Clinton campaign tried to divert the news from her unethical activities and blamed Russia for hacking and releasing the e-mails in order to make Clinton look bad. They said the Republicans did it to help her opponent Republican Presidential Nominee Donald Trump.

On July 10, 2016, Seth Rich, a worker for the Democratic National Committee was murdered by several gunshot wounds in his back. Whoever murdered Rich did not take his phone, watch or wallet. Julian Assange of *WikiLeaks*, released information strongly implying it was Seth Rich, not, Russia, who released the damaging Clinton emails and said Rich was killed while on his way to meet with the F.B.I. to discuss the wrongdoings by Hillary Clinton and Democrat Party leaders.

More than other 30 people have mysteriously died over the years, who had connections to Hillary Clinton and her husband, President Bill Clinton. Many conspiracy theories link the deaths to the Clintons. Some of them place the number of Clinton connected deaths at more than 90. The Clintons, and their defenders, claim all those deaths, are merely a coincidence. You need to look closely at the details and decide if the theories about the Clinton connection are myths or if they are possibly true.

Hopefully the alarming fact that some people involved in politics get hurt and die will not discourage you from getting involved in politics.

15.   Watch Out for Coercion.

Down through the ages there have always been people who tried to intimidate people not to vote, or to vote for their candidate.

Before and during the War Between the States, the Democrat Party's platform was pro-slavery. The Republican Party was founded to abolish slavery. Its' first presidential candidate, Abraham Lincoln was elected President of the United States. While President, Lincoln abolished slavery. The Republican-controlled Senate followed suit, passing the 13th Amendment.

51

In 1867, the Republican-controlled Congress passed the *Military Reconstruction Act*, which gave the vote to former slaves in 10 former slave states. In 1868, the Republicans put forward the 14th Amendment which granted every native-born citizen the right to vote. It was opposed by Democrats because it allowed former slaves the right to vote. African-Americans, began to vote in great numbers. Most of them voted Republican and elected African American Congressmen and Senators. By 1872, there were 320 African Americans serving in State and Federal Legislatures. A concentrated effort was made to stop African Americans from voting. Many Democrats were leaders in the Ku Klux Klan (KKK). The Klan murdered and physically intimidated African American voters for the next 100 years. Democrats also passed the infamous *Jim Crow Laws*, which made it difficult for African Americans to vote.

Voter Coercion also took place in the north against a different group of people. Many Irish Americans, immigrated to America and quickly became citizens. When they went to vote in New York City, they found *thugs*, born in America who called themselves *Native Americans*, outside the polling places turning them away. People like James *"Jimmy"* Corcoran, one of my great-grandfathers, gathered their own *thugs*, and made sure the Irish were allowed to vote.

Many Labor Unions were originally formed to protect workers, but after a while they often became political machines, backing a specific slate of candidates and encouraging their members to vote for them. The problem was they often used intimidation and coercion. One of the most notorious strongholds of political corruption was the Democrat Party political center known as *Tammany Hall* in New York City. My 1st great grandfather, John H. Maxwell, was Vice President of

Big 6, The International Typographical Printers Union, one of the most powerful unions associated with *Tammany Hall*.

Many Labor Unions still continue the practice of backing a specific slate of candidates and *strongly encouraging* their members to vote for them. I was at a demonstration, conducted by one union, outside of *David Letterman's Tonight Show* in New York City, when Republican George W. Bush was running for president. Bush was appearing that evening on the show with David Letterman. I had a good conversation, at the demonstration, with some of the union members about George W. Bush and his opponent Democrat candidate Al Gore. Two New York City Detectives came and escorted me away. They told me to look quickly over my shoulder. They said the men who were approaching me were union thugs who were about to rough me up for what I was saying. They told me they had probably just saved my life.

During the 2008 and 2012 Presidential Elections, it was reported a group, known as the *Black Panthers,* had its members stand outside of polling places in Philadelphia, intimidating voters from voting for anyone other than Barack Hussein Obama.

16.   Separation of Church & State.

Opponents of Religious Freedom have tried to silence religious people by using what they call the *Separation of Church and State argument.* They claim the Constitution contains the *Separation of Church and State* clause, with the intent that religion should play no part in government or public life. They have used that argument to remove God from schools, public buildings, public meeting places, the military and in any other place they can get it removed.

There are a few problems with their argument. First of all, the words, *Separation of Church and State* does not appear in the Constitution.

On October 7, 1801, the *Danbury Baptist Association*, wrote a congratulatory letter to Thomas Jefferson, the newly elected President of the United States. Baptists feared the strength of a strong central government, something Thomas Jefferson also opposed. They wrote to President Jefferson expressing their concern that the *"free exercise of religion,"* clause in the Constitution, might be viewed as a government-given right, rather than an inalienable right. They asked Jefferson to help protect the rights of minority religions, such as theirs.

Jefferson responded with a letter, in which stated that religious expression was a *"natural right"* of man, and the guarantee of the free exercise of religion in the Constitution built *"a wall of separation between the Church and State."* He assured them the State would not interfere with the Church.

The phrase, *Separation of Church and State*, which Jefferson used in his letter was drastically taken out of context and totally turned around in the last half of the 20th Century. It was made to mean the complete opposite of what Jefferson intended,

There are two clauses in the Constitution related to religion. The first is found in the First Amendment. It is called *the Establishment Clause*. It states, *"Congress shall make no law respecting an establishment of religion."*

The Constitution forbids the government from *establishing* a national church. The British Government tried to do that and it was one of the factors which caused the Revolutionary War.

Religious Freedom was the principle Roger Williams, and his fellow Baptists, invoked when they established Rhode Island. They forbid any state established church and welcomed other religious groups, such as Quakers and Jews. The first Jewish synagogue was founded in Newport, Rhode Island, with the support of the Baptists. The Founding Fathers followed their example when they drafted the Constitution.

The second clause, in the Constitution related to religion, says, *"or prohibiting the free exercise thereof."* That is known as *the Free Exercise Clause.* The Constitution forbade government from restricting the free exercise of religion. Yet many judges, politicians and their supporters, have done just that very thing, and continue to seek to do that. They would like to silence religious people.

17.   You Do Not Have to Say How You Voted.

Who you vote for is a private matter. You do not have to tell anyone who you voted for. When you cast your vote, either in present or by Absentee Ballot, it is a private matter. No one is to be able to see or know for whom you vote. It is a matter of public record that you voted, but no public record exists which shows how you voted.

There are some people who may pressure you to tell them how you voted. You may tell them if you want, but you do not have to tell anyone if or how you voted.

18.   Understand a Candidate's Philosophy.

One area of utmost importance, which many people fail to consider, is determining a Candidate's Philosophy. Everyone has a basic philosophy of life. That philosophy guides their actions. You must understand a Candidate's Philosophy. This is addressed in detail in the next section.

19.   The United States Constitution.

The United States Constitution is the *Rule of Law* in America. It is the standard, which each elected official swears to uphold when they take office. There are radically different views regarding how to interpret the Constitution. Those views will affect the actions a candidate will take, once in office.

It is very important to determine each candidate's view on how they believe we should interpret and apply the United States Constitution. This is addressed in detail in the next section.

Carefully Examine Each Candidate

Before you vote for a candidate you need to know some information about that candidate. The following are some important principles to consider.

1.   Vote for a Candidate, Not a Political Party.

It can be a good thing to belong to a political party. Political parties bring together people with common philosophies and policies. The overwhelming majority of people who are elected belong to a political party.

When you belong to a political party it allows you to vote in a primary for a candidate to represent your party.

It is important to remember, just because a candidate is elected to represent your party, they may not be a good person.

When my son Matt Maxwell, sought the nomination for his party in a congressional race in Connecticut, some of the town party committees, endorsed another candidate before hearing him or the other candidate. They would not even allow him or the other candidates to speak

Some political parties choose the candidates they will endorse, because of past political favors granted. Democrats have what they call *Super Delegates* who can vote for whoever they want, during a Presidential Campaign. During the 2016 Presidential campaign many of those *Super Delegates* pledged their support to Hillary Clinton before primaries were held in their state. Some such as Elizabeth Esty, Congresswoman for the 5th Connecticut Congressional District disregarded the will of her constituents and pledged her vote for Hillary Clinton, even though Sen. Bernie Sanders of Vermont won her district.

I strongly recommend you examine each candidate and vote for individuals. Do not just vote for a candidate because they belong to your political party. I always look at each candidate and have often voted for someone from a different political party because I believed they were the better candidate.

2.   Examine Their Platform.

Every candidate for any office should have lists available stating what they stand for. Those are usually called their *Platform* or *Position Papers*. Look at each candidate's positions carefully and see how they line up with your core beliefs.

It is not unusual for candidates running for local office to not mention a position on national issues. A candidate for school board will usually not indicate their position on issues such as abortion or the military. That does not mean you cannot ask them their positions on those or other issues.

Watch out for generic statements. Many candidates include statements in their platform such as: creating more jobs, providing tax cuts, education reform, more access to health care, and better treatment for our veterans. Those are general *"feel good"* statements many use. It does not really tell you what a candidate stands for or how a candidate will vote.

Look for more specifics. Make a list of issues which are important to you. Look to see if, and how, they are addressed in each candidate's plans. If they are not specifically addressed, ask them for their specific position and related plans.

Ask questions like: How do you specifically plan to create jobs? How do you plan to improve the economy? What specific tax cuts do you propose? What is your position regarding the rights of the unborn?

When my son Matt Maxwell was running for the United States Congress in Connecticut, he and two other candidates, seeking to secure the nomination from his party, spoke for a group of people in one of the cities in his district. They were asked the question, *"What will you do for our city?'*

The first candidate, said he would find out what was important to them and seek to represent them in Congress. The second candidate issued a similar answer. That is the way most politicians answer such questions.

My son answered their question in a different way. He addressed the fact that there were large areas in the city, where once productive factories stood, which were now vacant. He outlined a specific plan as to how he would put those building back into production, thus creating new jobs.

One good source to find a candidate's platform is to look at Voter Guides, which are put out by various groups. Make sure they are valid Voter Guides, not bogus Voter Guides put together by some groups to make a candidate look bad. It is a good idea to look at the Voter Guides from groups you agree with and those you disagree with.

Some Sources for Voters Guides include:

- AARP.org - American Association of Retired Persons
- AAUWAction.org – American Association of University Women
- Action.NAACP.org – National Association for the Advancement of Colored People
- AFAAction.net – American Family Association Action

○ Ballotpedia,org – Listing of State Issued Voter Guides
○ CC.org – Christian Coalition of America
○ ChristianVoterGuide.com
○ FRC.org = Family Research Council
○ LVW.org – League of Women Voters
○ NRAPVF.org – National Rifle Association
○ WallBuilders.com – Conservative Christian

3.   Determine Their View on Specific Issues.

Though a candidate's platform may address a number of issues, which concern you, there are some they may specifically not address, for fear their position will alienate some voters.

The following are some issues a number of Candidates have strong views about. A number of these issues overlap. It is a good idea to know a candidate's position on each of these items to see if you are comfortable with their view:

○ Abortion – Right to Life or Right to Terminate a Life
○ Assisted Suicide – Right to Die
○ Crime – Punishment & Rehabilitation
○ Drugs – Legalization, Punishment & Treatment
○ Education - School Choice & Common Core
○ Economy – Capitalist or Socialist, Free Enterprise
○ Energy & Alternative Energy – Oil & Fracking
○ Environmental Issues – Are they an Environmentalist or Conservationist?
○ Gambling – Lotteries & Casinos
○ Gun Ownership & Regulation – The 2nd Amendment
○ Health Care – Private or Government
○ Immigration Issues – Border Control
○ International Relations – United Nations
○ Israel – Our Relationship with Israel

O LGBT Issues

O Marriage & the Family – What is Marriage?

O Medical Research – Funding & Moral Limits

O Military – Who should Serve, International Intervention

O Minimum Wage

O Religion – Freedom *of* or Freedom *from* Religion

O Space Exploration – Funding & Plans

O State's Rights vs. Federal Jurisdiction

O Taxation – Raise or Lower Taxes, View on Flat Rate

O Term Limits – Yes or No

O Terrorism – Who is the Enemy & How to Stop Them

O Voter Registration – Photo Identification or not?

O Women's Issues – Such as Equal Pay

4.   Examine Their Philosophy.

Everyone has some basic philosophy of life. Your philosophy of life guides your actions. Though some people may not be able to explain their philosophy of life, those running for political office should be able to clearly explain their philosophy. When you understand a candidate's philosophy it can help you get a good idea of how they may make decisions on various issues.

Though there are many different schools of philosophy, most of the ones related to politics, fall under one of two categories: *The Humanistic Philosophy of Situational Ethics* or the *Philosophy of Moral Absolutism.*

O **The Philosophy of Moral Absolutism** - Many people used to follow the philosophy of *Moral Absolutism*. That was the view of almost all of the Founding Fathers of America. That view has fallen out of favor with many people, especially those in many institutions of higher learning. Those who hold to this

61

philosophy will view things as morally right or wrong, no matter what the desired outcome is. For some of them, Society determines what is morally right or wrong. For others, it is their God or Holy Book, which makes that determination. Many Conservative Christians, Orthodox Jews and Muslims hold to that philosophy. Many political conservatives also hold to this philosophy.

○ **The Humanistic Philosophy of Situational Ethics** - Many more people today follow the *Humanistic Philosophy of Situational Ethics*. That is the philosophy taught in most educational institutions. That philosophy basically believes you have to look at each situation to determine what action you will take to achieve your desired outcome. It does not pass moral judgment on actions as long as the positive desired outcome is achieved. This can also be called *Relativism*. For many adherents of this philosophy, the ends justify the means. This is the prevalent philosophy among people who are more politically liberal.

Determine which philosophy you follow and makes sure the candidates you choose have that same philosophy.

5.   Determine Their View on the Constitution.

It is important to determine a candidate's view on the United States Constitution, especially if they are running for state or national office.   The United States Constitution is both the founding and guiding document for our government.

Many people do not realize there are radically different views about how the Constitution is to be interpreted. The view a candidate holds about the Constitution will affect their policies and procedures and their stand on a number of issues.

○ **Original Intent** – This view of the Constitution looks at the Constitution like an unchanging solid rock, which sets forth clear principles, which must be interpreted literally, based on the writer's *Original Intent*, and must then be followed. Those who follow this view believe the Constitution contains within it means for change, but those changes must be done by amendments proposed by elected Senators, and then ratified by the states. One of the best places to learn what the Founding Fathers meant, when they wrote the Constitution, is to read what they said about it. One of the best sources is the *Federalist Papers*, written by Alexander Hamilton, James Madison and John Jay.

○ **Fluid Document** - Many people look at the Constitution as a living, *Fluid Document* whose meaning changes with time. They say we cannot be bound by a document written when slavery was legal and women could not vote. They believe the Supreme Court has the right to decide what the Constitution means, even if its decisions are in conflict with the Founding Father's original intent.

A person's view of how to interpret the Constitution will affect the way a candidate views various core principles contained in the Constitution.

Consider the *Second Amendment*. Those who look at the Constitution as a **Fluid Document** often state the reason for the Second Amendment was because America had just gone through a war with England and people felt the need to have weapons to defend themselves. Some of those same people will say it was included so people could have a weapon to use for hunting. They will argue that today, people no longer need weapons to protect themselves. They claim weapons have become more dangerous and should not be owned by the average citizen. They argue strongly that the *Second Amendment* never meant people should be allowed to own what they call *military-style assault weapons*. They argue, that if people do own guns, those guns should be restricted to their own homes or only allowed on a regulated firing range or only be used when hunting.

Those who hold to the historical ***Original Intent*** view of the Constitution argue that the *Second Amendment* says citizens are allowed to *bear arms*, which means to carry them with them. They point out it does not say anything about hunting. They may point out how the first battle in the Revolutionary War occurred when the British government sought to disarm the colonists Some will point to the writings of Thomas Jefferson, one of the Founding Fathers, who explained the reason to have armed citizens was in case the government became intrusive. They may point out that the weapons, the citizens were allowed to own and carry with them, were ones such as the Brown Bess Musket, a 75-caliber *military assault weapon*. They point out that the *Original Intent* of the Constitution, derived from the Founding Fathers own writing, was that the citizens were allowed to be armed with the same military weapons as the government.

6.   Examine Their Track Record.

When I look at a candidate, I want to know, what have they done. Many candidates are good talkers, but have done little. Many candidates have been politicians all of their lives. Most of them had someone else pay their way through school. They never had to work to earn money, or never had to pay their own rent or mortgage. Most candidates never experienced what it is to hold a 9-to-5 job, nor ever had a blue collar job in their life.

Many candidates also never had any real community service. They may have helped on a political campaign or with some committee but most never physically volunteered helping others in a meaningful way for more than a day or two at a time.

When I was the founder and president of *Habitat for Humanity* in Putnam County, New York, we had our share of politicians who would show up for a photo opportunity. Some just held a hammer for a picture. Some stayed for 5, 10 or maybe as long as 20 minutes, but few stayed for an hour and only a handful came and really worked for any length of time, especially if no reporters or photographers were present.

Find out what are the specific types of community service a Candidate has participated in and what kind of paying jobs has a candidate held?

One way to check out a candidate's track record is to do an internet search for the candidate's name. One of the problems in doing an internet search is some search engines, such as *Yahoo* and *Google* have been known to edit search results so it limits positive responses on conservative candidates.

As you conduct an internet search, you must understand everything you read on the internet is not true. Some people set up websites with false information about candidates to mislead those doing internet searches. Some extremist groups set up websites supporting their candidate with erroneous information about them, or about their opponent, in order to make their candidate look good and their opponent look bad.

You can do a newspaper search to see what articles mention them by name. Many local libraries have digital images of local newspapers, which you can search. Be sure to look for older, as well as more recent, articles.

If a candidate has served in the United States Senate or House of Representatives, their attendance and voting record can be find in the *Congressional Record*. You really should look at that.

Some Voter Guides may give you some helpful background information about a candidate, especially if they have already served in some elected position.

7.   Look at Who a Candidate Associates With.

You can tell a lot about a person by the people they associate with. I had a wise professor who taught us, *"we become the books we read and the people we associate with."*

The Old Testament Scriptures gives some good advice about who you associate with. It says, *do not go with an angry man.* It also says, *a companion of wise men will be wise but a companion of fools will be destroyed.*

We had a very hateful politician in our area who was eventually exposed for being a corrupt politician. He had to give up his re-election bid and then fled the state. He reminded me of Adolf Hitler. When candidates for elected office asked me for their endorsement, I always asked them what was their relationship with that politician? I did not let on how I felt. Their response told me a lot about them. One candidate told me the disgraced former Senator was his mentor. That helped me know that candidate was keeping bad company and would not be getting my vote.

Understand the Role & Purpose of The Three Branches of Government

It is very important to understand our Founding Fathers established a government which divided power between three distinct branches of government. They established checks and balances, so one branch of government cannot become more powerful than the others. Many politicians cross those lines and would like to eliminate that clear division of power.

1. Legislative Branch.

The Legislative Branch of government makes the laws and has authority to approve or reject the budget, submitted by the President. They also are the only ones with authority to declare war and to establish taxes to fund the government.

The Legislative Branch is divided into two bodies of elected officials: The Senate and the House of Representatives.

In the Senate, each state gets two Senators, so each state has equal representation. That helps give a state with a small population the same power as a state with a large population.

Senators must be at least 30 years old. They are elected to serve for a six-year term. Currently there is no limit on the number of terms a Senator may serve. The terms of the two Senators in a state expire different years.

In the House of Representatives, representation is based on population. That population is based on the United States Census, which is taken every 10 years. Each state is divided into congressional districts based on population. A state with a small population will have less congressional representatives than a state with a larger population.

Members of the House of Representatives are called congressmen, even if they are women. Some of the women elected to the House of Representatives identify themselves as *congresswoman* and some use the term *congressman*. Some use the politically correct term, *congressperson*. No matter what you call them, they must be at least 25 years old. They are elected to serve a two-year term. Every one of them comes up for election every two years. There is no limit as to how many terms they may serve.

Laws may be proposed in either the Senate or the House of Representatives, but the laws must be passed by both the Senate and House to become a law.

Many politicians serving in the Senate or the House of Representatives try to become career politicians, staying in office as long as possible. The longer a politician stays in office, the more powerful they usually become. That is because they have usually earned enough favors from their fellow politicians to be able to pass more of their legislation. Many of them oppose term-limits.

One of the reasons many members of the Senate and House of Representatives oppose term limits, or want to make sure they can serve at least five years, is because they become eligible for a pension at the age of 62, if they have completed at least five years of service. Members are eligible for a pension at age 50 if they have completed 20 years of service, or at any age, after completing 25 years of service. The amount of the pension depends on years of service and the average of the highest three years of salary. By law, the starting amount of a Member's retirement payment may not exceed 80% of his or her final salary. The government will pay up to 75% of their health care premiums for the rest of their lives.

No wonder people want those positions, I do not know of any company which will pay you a retirement, which is 80% of your final salary, after only five years of service.

2. Executive Branch.

The Executive Branch of the United States Government is given the responsibility to represent the county but primarily to run the day-to-day business of the country. It comprised of the President and the Vice President.

The President must be a native-born citizen of the United States and must be at least 35 years old on the day he is sworn into office. The President is elected to a four-year term. A President may be elected to serve two four-year terms or a total of 10 years. The 10-year provision is in case the person becomes President mid-term. That can happen if the person was Vice President and the President they served under was unable to fulfill their full-term. After that, they could then run for two full four-year terms.

The President is the Chief Executive Officer of the United States. The President's main duty is to administer the operation of the country. They must be someone with good business and administrative skills.

The other duty of the President is to represent the United States, domestically and internationally. As the lead representative of the country, it can help if the President is a dynamic, out-going, inspiring person with good diplomatic and people skills.

The President also serves of Commander-in-Chief of the nation's military. The first President of the United States had military experience, as did 22 other Presidents.

A serious problem is, most people choose a President based on their personality, rather on their administrative skills. That has resulted in some very ineffective Presidents.

The President has one of the best retirement packages in the world. The retirement benefits received by former Presidents include a pension, Secret Service protection, health care, and reimbursements for staff, travel, mail, and office expenses for life. The Presidential pension is not a fixed amount, rather it matches the current salary of Cabinet members (or Executive Level I personnel), which was $205,700 per year as of 2016. What other job gives a retirement package like that after only four years of service?

3.   Judicial Branch.

The Judicial Branch of the government is given the responsibility to see that the laws of the country are upheld and enforced. They have no authority to modify or establish any law.

The Supreme Court is the highest court in the land. The judges are nominated by the President of the United States and approved by a majority vote of the Senate. Presidents usually choose judges who share their philosophy.

There are no official requirements regarding age in the Constitution regarding Supreme Court Justices. They are appointed for life, unless removed from office.

Supreme Court Justices can have a tremendous influence, either good or bad. Most judges, try to make their retirement coincide with the term of a President, who holds to their same philosophy, in order to assure their successor continues to make the same kind of decisions they would make.

Some die before they plan to retire, which allows the President, to put forward a successor. That successor may have a totally different philosophy than the justice who died and could alter the decision made by the court.

The job of the Supreme Court is to see that the laws established by the Legislative Branch are in agreement with the Constitution and that they are upheld and enforced. It has no authority to establish law.

America has a very serious problem. Many of the judges on the Supreme Court violate the Constitution and establish laws with their rulings. Such judges should be removed from the bench but that is seldom done.

Section 1 of Article 3 in the Constitution says a Supreme Court Justice may hold their term, *"during good behavior."* That means, if it is ever determine they do not have *"good behavior,"* they should be removed from office. There is an impeachment procedure in the Constitution for their removal.

Retiring U.S. Supreme Court justices are entitled to receive a lifetime pension which is equal to their highest full salary. In order to qualify for the full pension, retiring justices must have served for a minimum of 10 years, provided the sum of the justice's age and years of Supreme Court service totals 80.

The fact that Supreme Court Justices serve for such a long time, and because their decisions can greatly affect the entire country, one of the most important considerations you should make, when considering a candidate for President is, what type of Supreme Court Justices will they appoint?

Understand the Duties of an Elected Office

It is important to elect people who can do a good job in the office they are seeking to fill, rather than to elect someone who is popular. Too many times people vote for candidate because they are popular. Some popular candidates get elected but are unable to do a good job because they lack the necessary skills or qualifications.

The skills required to do a good job as an elected official do not necessarily require a college education. Formal education may be helpful but experience and some other qualifications are more helpful. There are different skill sets required for different elected positions. You need to understand the duties of a specific position so you can then determine if a candidate has the necessary background or experience to effectively fill that position.

Most elected positions fall into one of two categories; they are either Administrative or Non-Administrative.

1.   Administrative Elected Positions

Administrative positions are ones which require the person to do daily administrative duties. That would be similar to an executive in a company.

Some Administrative Elected Positions include President of the United States, Governor of a State, County Executive, and Mayor or Supervisor of a Town.

A candidate seeking any of those administrative position should have a good background and skills in administration.

Someone who served as a Governor may have a good set of skills or experience, which could help them become a good President. Seventeen Presidents of the United States served first as Governors of States.

Having served as a Senator or in as a Member of the House of Representatives is not enough of a qualification to become President. Those positions require very different skill sets.

2. Non-Administrative Elected Positions

Some elected positions are non-administrative. Though the elected official may have a staff and may sit on various committees, the elected official in those non-administrative positions does not administer or run anything in the government. Their main function is to represent their state or area.

Both Senators and Members of the House of Representatives are non-administrative positions. The same is true of most State Senators or State Assembly Members. Though it does not hurt for them to have administrative skills, those candidates do not need an administrative background.

They need good persuasive skills, as their main function is to make sure their state or region is effectively represented. They will have to be able to negotiate and convince other representatives to pass their bills. They are really more like a salesman than an executive.

This does not mean someone with administrative skills and background could not make a good Senator or Congressperson, but they must have the good persuasive skills.

Make sure you select a candidate with the appropriate skill set and experience the position they desire requires.

Conclusion

Hopefully this book has helped you see the importance of voting and hopefully you will heed the warnings presented herein.

There are many bad people involved in politics, you must be very careful. Do not get discouraged, there are also some good people out there. Perhaps you should encourage someone you know, who stands for the things you support, to run for office. Do not be afraid of political parties who do not listen to you. Do not let Power Brokers and all the corruption discourage you. Good can overcome evil.

Look carefully at each Candidate. When I am looking at candidates I claim a promise I found in the New Testament. The Apostle James said, *If you lack wisdom, ask God and He will give it to you.* I pray that prayer a lot.

It is possible you may not find a candidate you fully agree with. In some cases, you may find little common ground between you and any of the candidates. It may appear all you have is a choice between two evils. If you find yourself in that situation, make sure you still vote. You must choose the one who stands for, what you believe are the better principles, otherwise your non-vote may very likely elect the worst candidate.

After an election, be sure to hold the elected candidates accountable. Pray for them. Encourage them to make good decisions and congratulate them in writing when they do.

Make sure you are informed, before you vote, and then go make a difference with your vote!

Appendix 1
The Declaration of Independence

In Congress, July 4, 1776
A Declaration
By the Representative of The
United States of America,
In General Congress Assembled

When in the Course of human events, it becomes necessary for one people to dissolve the political bands which have connected them with another, and to assume among the powers of the earth, the separate and equal station to which the Laws of Nature and of Nature's God entitle them, a decent respect to the opinions of mankind requires that they should declare the causes which impel them to the separation.

We hold these truths to be self-evident, that all men are created equal, that they are endowed by their Creator with certain unalienable Rights, that among these are Life, Liberty and the pursuit of Happiness.--That to secure these rights, Governments are instituted among Men, deriving their just powers from the consent of the governed, --That whenever any Form of Government becomes destructive of these ends, it is the Right of the People to alter or to abolish it, and to institute new Government, laying its foundation on such principles and organizing its powers in such form, as to them shall seem most likely to effect their Safety and Happiness. Prudence, indeed, will dictate that Governments long established should not be changed for light and transient causes; and accordingly all experience hath shewn, that mankind are more disposed to suffer, while evils are sufferable, than to right themselves by abolishing the forms to which they are accustomed. But when a long train of abuses and usurpations, pursuing invariably the same Object evinces a design to reduce them under absolute Despotism, it is their right, it is their duty, to throw off such Government, and to provide new Guards for their future security. Such has been the patient sufferance of these Colonies; and such is now the necessity which constrains them to alter their former Systems of Government. The history of the present King of Great-Britain is a history of repeated injuries and usurpations, all having in direct object the establishment of an absolute Tyranny over these States. To prove this, let Facts be submitted to a candid world.

He has refused his Assent to Laws, the most wholesome and necessary for the public good.

He has forbidden his Governors to pass Laws of immediate and pressing importance, unless suspended in their operation till his Assent should be obtained; and when so suspended, he has utterly neglected to attend to them.

He has refused to pass other Laws for the accommodation of large districts of people, unless those people would relinquish the right of Representation in the Legislature, a right inestimable to them and formidable to tyrants only.

He has called together legislative bodies at places unusual, uncomfortable, and distant from the depository of their public Records, for the sole purpose of fatiguing them into compliance with his measures.

He has dissolved Representative Houses repeatedly, for opposing with manly firmness his invasions on the rights of the people.

He has refused for a long time, after such dissolutions, to cause others to be elected; whereby the Legislative powers, incapable of Annihilation, have returned to the People at large for their exercise; the State remaining in the mean time exposed to all the dangers of invasion from without, and convulsions within.

He has endeavoured to prevent the population of these States; for that purpose obstructing the Laws for Naturalization of Foreigners; refusing to pass others to encourage their migrations hither, and raising the conditions of new Appropriations of Lands.

He has obstructed the Administration of Justice, by refusing his Assent to Laws for establishing Judiciary powers.

He has made Judges dependent on his Will alone, for the tenure of their offices, and the amount and payment of their salaries.

He has erected a multitude of New Offices, and sent hither swarms of Officers to harrass our people, and eat out their substance.

He has kept among us, in times of peace, Standing Armies without the Consent of our legislatures.

He has affected to render the Military independent of and superior to the Civil power.

He has combined with others to subject us to a jurisdiction foreign to our constitution, and unacknowledged by our laws; giving his Assent to their Acts of pretended Legislation:

For Quartering large bodies of armed troops among us:

For protecting them, by a mock Trial, from punishment for any Murders which they should commit on the Inhabitants of these States:

For cutting off our Trade with all parts of the world:

For imposing Taxes on us without our Consent:

For depriving us in many cases, of the benefits of Trial by Jury:

For transporting us beyond Seas to be tried for pretended offences

For abolishing the free System of English Laws in a neighbouring Province, establishing therein an Arbitrary government, and enlarging its Boundaries so as to render it at once an example and fit instrument for introducing the same absolute rule into these Colonies:

For taking away our Charters, abolishing our most valuable Laws, and

altering fundamentally the Forms of our Governments:
For suspending our own Legislatures, and declaring themselves invested with power to legislate for us in all cases whatsoever.
He has abdicated Government here, by declaring us out of his Protection and waging War against us.
He has plundered our seas, ravaged our Coasts, burnt our towns, and destroyed the lives of our people.
He is at this time transporting large Armies of foreign Mercenaries to compleat the works of death, desolation and tyranny, already begun with circumstances of Cruelty & perfidy scarcely paralleled in the most barbarous ages, and totally unworthy the Head of a civilized nation.
He has constrained our fellow Citizens taken Captive on the high Seas to bear Arms against their Country, to become the executioners of their friends and Brethren, or to fall themselves by their Hands.
He has excited domestic insurrections amongst us, and has endeavoured to bring on the inhabitants of our frontiers, the merciless Indian Savages, whose known rule of warfare, is an undistinguished destruction of all ages, sexes and conditions.
In every stage of these Oppressions We have Petitioned for Redress in the most humble terms: Our repeated Petitions have been answered only by repeated injury. A Prince whose character is thus marked by every act which may define a Tyrant, is unfit to be the ruler of a free people.
Nor have We been wanting in attentions to our British brethren. We have warned them from time to time of attempts by their legislature to extend an unwarrantable jurisdiction over us. We have reminded them of the circumstances of our emigration and settlement here. We have appealed to their native justice and magnanimity, and we have conjured them by the ties of our common kindred to disavow these usurpations, which, would inevitably interrupt our connections and correspondence. They too have been deaf to the voice of justice and of consanguinity. We must, therefore, acquiesce in the necessity, which denounces our Separation, and hold them, as we hold the rest of mankind, Enemies in War, in Peace Friends.
We, therefore, the Representatives of the united States of America, in General Congress, Assembled, appealing to the Supreme Judge of the world for the rectitude of our intentions, do, in the Name, and by Authority of the good People of these Colonies, solemnly publish and declare, That these United Colonies are, and of Right ought to be Free and Independent States; that they are Absolved from all Allegiance to the British Crown, and that all political connection between them and the State of Great Britain, is and ought to be totally dissolved; and that as Free and Independent States, they have full Power to levy War, conclude Peace, contract Alliances, establish Commerce, and to do all other Acts and Things which Independent States may of right do. And

for the support of this Declaration, with a firm reliance on the protection of divine Providence, we mutually pledge to each other our Lives, our Fortunes and our sacred Honor.
Signed By Order and in Behalf of The Congress,
John Hancock, President.
Attest Charles Thomson, Secretary.

Signed by the Following:
Georgia: Button Gwinnett, Lyman Hall, George Walton
North Carolina: William Hooper, Joseph Hewes, John Penn
South Carolina: Edward Rutledge, Thomas Heyward, Jr., Thomas Lynch, Jr., Arthur Middleton
Massachusetts: John Hancock
Maryland: Samuel Chase, William Paca, Thomas Stone, Charles Carroll of Carrollton
Virginia: George Wythe, Richard Henry Lee, Thomas Jefferson, Benjamin Harrison, Thomas Nelson, Jr., Francis Lightfoot Lee, Carter Braxton
Pennsylvania: Robert Morris, Benjamin Rush, Benjamin Franklin, John Morton, George Clymer, James Smith, George Taylor, James Wilson, George Ross
Delaware: Caesar Rodney, George Read, Thomas McKean
New York: William Floyd, Philip Livingston, Francis Lewis, Lewis Morris
New Jersey: Richard Stockton, John Witherspoon, Francis Hopkinson, John Hart, Abraham Clark
New Hampshire: Josiah Bartlett, William Whipple
Massachusetts: Samuel Adams, John Adams, Robert Treat Paine, Elbridge Gerry
Rhode Island: Stephen Hopkins, William Ellery
Connecticut: Roger Sherman, Samuel Huntington, William Williams, Oliver Wolcott
New Hampshire: Matthew Thornton

Appendix 2
The Constitution of the United States of America

We the People of the United States, in Order to form a more perfect Union, establish Justice, insure domestic Tranquility, provide for the common defence, promote the general Welfare, and secure the Blessings of Liberty to ourselves and our Posterity, do ordain and establish this Constitution for the United States of America.

Article. I.

Section. 1. All legislative Powers herein granted shall be vested in a Congress of the United States, which shall consist of a Senate and House of Representatives.

Section. 2. The House of Representatives shall be composed of Members chosen every second Year by the People of the several States, and the Electors in each State shall have the Qualifications requisite for Electors of the most numerous Branch of the State Legislature.

No Person shall be a Representative who shall not have attained to the Age of twenty five Years, and been seven Years a Citizen of the United States, and who shall not, when elected, be an Inhabitant of that State in which he shall be chosen.

Representatives and direct Taxes shall be apportioned among the several States which may be included within this Union, according to their respective Numbers, which shall be determined by adding to the whole Number of free Persons, including those bound to Service for a Term of Years, and excluding Indians not taxed, three fifths of all other Persons. The actual Enumeration shall be made within three Years after the first Meeting of the Congress of the United States, and within every subsequent Term of ten Years, in such Manner as they shall by Law direct. The Number of Representatives shall not exceed one for every thirty Thousand, but each State shall have at Least one Representative; and until such enumeration shall be made, the State of New Hampshire shall be entitled to chuse three, Massachusetts eight, Rhode-Island and Providence Plantations one, Connecticut five, New-York six, New Jersey four, Pennsylvania eight, Delaware one, Maryland six, Virginia ten, North Carolina five, South Carolina five, and Georgia three.

When vacancies happen in the Representation from any State, the Executive Authority thereof shall issue Writs of Election to fill such Vacancies.

The House of Representatives shall chuse their Speaker and other Officers; and shall have the sole Power of Impeachment.

Section. 3. The Senate of the United States shall be composed of two Senators from each State, chosen by the Legislature thereof, for six Years; and each Senator shall have one Vote.
Immediately after they shall be assembled in Consequence of the first Election, they shall be divided as equally as may be into three Classes. The Seats of the Senators of the first Class shall be vacated at the Expiration of the second Year, of the second Class at the Expiration of the fourth Year, and of the third Class at the Expiration of the sixth Year, so that one third may be chosen every second Year; and if Vacancies happen by Resignation, or otherwise, during the Recess of the Legislature of any State, the Executive thereof may make temporary Appointments until the next Meeting of the Legislature, which shall then fill such Vacancies.
No Person shall be a Senator who shall not have attained to the Age of thirty Years, and been nine Years a Citizen of the United States, and who shall not, when elected, be an Inhabitant of that State for which he shall be chosen.
The Vice President of the United States shall be President of the Senate, but shall have no Vote, unless they be equally divided.
The Senate shall chuse their other Officers, and also a President pro tempore, in the Absence of the Vice President, or when he shall exercise the Office of President of the United States.
The Senate shall have the sole Power to try all Impeachments. When sitting for that Purpose, they shall be on Oath or Affirmation. When the President of the United States is tried, the Chief Justice shall preside: And no Person shall be convicted without the Concurrence of two thirds of the Members present.
Judgment in Cases of Impeachment shall not extend further than to removal from Office, and disqualification to hold and enjoy any Office of honor, Trust or Profit under the United States: but the Party convicted shall nevertheless be liable and subject to Indictment, Trial, Judgment and Punishment, according to Law.
Section. 4. The Times, Places and Manner of holding Elections for Senators and Representatives, shall be prescribed in each State by the Legislature thereof; but the Congress may at any time by Law make or alter such Regulations, except as to the Places of chusing Senators.
The Congress shall assemble at least once in every Year, and such Meeting shall be on the first Monday in December, unless they shall by Law appoint a different Day.
Section. 5. Each House shall be the Judge of the Elections, Returns and Qualifications of its own Members, and a Majority of each shall constitute a Quorum to do Business; but a smaller Number may adjourn from day to day, and may be authorized to compel the Attendance of

absent Members, in such Manner, and under such Penalties as each House may provide.

Each House may determine the Rules of its Proceedings, punish its Members for disorderly Behaviour, and, with the Concurrence of two thirds, expel a Member.

Each House shall keep a Journal of its Proceedings, and from time to time publish the same, excepting such Parts as may in their Judgment require Secrecy; and the Yeas and Nays of the Members of either House on any question shall, at the Desire of one fifth of those Present, be entered on the Journal.

Neither House, during the Session of Congress, shall, without the Consent of the other, adjourn for more than three days, nor to any other Place than that in which the two Houses shall be sitting.

Section. 6. The Senators and Representatives shall receive a Compensation for their Services, to be ascertained by Law, and paid out of the Treasury of the United States. They shall in all Cases, except Treason, Felony and Breach of the Peace, be privileged from Arrest during their Attendance at the Session of their respective Houses, and in going to and returning from the same; and for any Speech or Debate in either House, they shall not be questioned in any other Place.

No Senator or Representative shall, during the Time for which he was elected, be appointed to any civil Office under the Authority of the United States, which shall have been created, or the Emoluments whereof shall have been encreased during such time; and no Person holding any Office under the United States, shall be a Member of either House during his Continuance in Office.

Section. 7. All Bills for raising Revenue shall originate in the House of Representatives; but the Senate may propose or concur with Amendments as on other Bills.

Every Bill which shall have passed the House of Representatives and the Senate, shall, before it become a Law, be presented to the President of the United States; If he approve he shall sign it, but if not he shall return it, with his Objections to that House in which it shall have originated, who shall enter the Objections at large on their Journal, and proceed to reconsider it. If after such Reconsideration two thirds of that House shall agree to pass the Bill, it shall be sent, together with the Objections, to the other House, by which it shall likewise be reconsidered, and if approved by two thirds of that House, it shall become a Law. But in all such Cases the Votes of both Houses shall be determined by yeas and Nays, and the Names of the Persons voting for and against the Bill shall be entered on the Journal of each House respectively. If any Bill shall not be returned by the President within ten Days (Sundays excepted) after it shall have been presented to him, the Same shall be a Law, in like Manner as if he had signed it, unless the Congress by their Adjournment prevent its Return, in which Case it shall not be a Law. Every Order, Resolution, or Vote to which the Concurrence of the Senate and House of Representatives may be necessary (except on a question of Adjournment) shall be presented to the President of the United States; and before the Same shall take Effect, shall be approved by him, or being disapproved by him, shall be repassed by two thirds of the Senate and House of Representatives, according to the Rules and Limitations prescribed in the Case of a Bill.

Section. 8. The Congress shall have Power To lay and collect Taxes, Duties, Imposts and Excises, to pay the Debts and provide for the common Defence and general Welfare of the United States; but all Duties, Imposts and Excises shall be uniform throughout the United States;

To borrow Money on the credit of the United States;

To regulate Commerce with foreign Nations, and among the several States, and with the Indian Tribes;

To establish an uniform Rule of Naturalization, and uniform Laws on the subject of Bankruptcies throughout the United States;

To coin Money, regulate the Value thereof, and of foreign Coin, and fix the Standard of Weights and Measures;

To provide for the Punishment of counterfeiting the Securities and current Coin of the United States;

To establish Post Offices and post Roads;

To promote the Progress of Science and useful Arts, by securing for limited Times to Authors and Inventors the exclusive Right to their respective Writings and Discoveries;

To constitute Tribunals inferior to the supreme Court;

To define and punish Piracies and Felonies committed on the high Seas, and Offences against the Law of Nations;

To declare War, grant Letters of Marque and Reprisal, and make Rules concerning Captures on Land and Water;

To raise and support Armies, but no Appropriation of Money to that Use shall be for a longer Term than two Years;

To provide and maintain a Navy;

To make Rules for the Government and Regulation of the land and naval Forces;

To provide for calling forth the Militia to execute the Laws of the Union, suppress Insurrections and repel Invasions;

To provide for organizing, arming, and disciplining, the Militia, and for governing such Part of them as may be employed in the Service of the United States, reserving to the States respectively, the Appointment of the Officers, and the Authority of training the Militia according to the discipline prescribed by Congress;

To exercise exclusive Legislation in all Cases whatsoever, over such District (not exceeding ten Miles square) as may, by Cession of particular States, and the Acceptance of Congress, become the Seat of the Government of the United States, and to exercise like Authority over all Places purchased by the Consent of the Legislature of the State in which the Same shall be, for the Erection of Forts, Magazines, Arsenals, dock-Yards, and other needful Buildings;—And To make all Laws which shall be necessary and proper for carrying into Execution the foregoing Powers, and all other Powers vested by this Constitution in the Government of the United States, or in any Department or Officer thereof.

Section. 9. The Migration or Importation of such Persons as any of the States now existing shall think proper to admit, shall not be prohibited by the Congress prior to the Year one thousand eight hundred and eight, but a Tax or duty may be imposed on such Importation, not exceeding ten dollars for each Person.

The Privilege of the Writ of Habeas Corpus shall not be suspended, unless when in Cases of Rebellion or Invasion the public Safety may require it.

No Bill of Attainder or ex post facto Law shall be passed.

No Capitation, or other direct, Tax shall be laid, unless in Proportion to the Census or enumeration herein before directed to be taken.

No Tax or Duty shall be laid on Articles exported from any State.

No Preference shall be given by any Regulation of Commerce or Revenue to the Ports of one State over those of another: nor shall Vessels bound to, or from, one State, be obliged to enter, clear, or pay Duties in another.

No Money shall be drawn from the Treasury, but in Consequence of Appropriations made by Law; and a regular Statement and Account of the Receipts and Expenditures of all public Money shall be published from time to time.

No Title of Nobility shall be granted by the United States: And no Person holding any Office of Profit or Trust under them, shall, without the Consent of the Congress, accept of any present, Emolument, Office, or Title, of any kind whatever, from any King, Prince, or foreign State.

Section. 10. No State shall enter into any Treaty, Alliance, or Confederation; grant Letters of Marque and Reprisal; coin Money; emit Bills of Credit; make any Thing but gold and silver Coin a Tender in Payment of Debts; pass any Bill of Attainder, ex post facto Law, or Law impairing the Obligation of Contracts, or grant any Title of Nobility.

No State shall, without the Consent of the Congress, lay any Imposts or Duties on Imports or Exports, except what may be absolutely necessary for executing it's inspection Laws: and the net Produce of all Duties and Imposts, laid by any State on Imports or Exports, shall be for the Use of the Treasury of the United States; and all such Laws shall be subject to the Revision and Controul of the Congress.

No State shall, without the Consent of Congress, lay any Duty of Tonnage, keep Troops, or Ships of War in time of Peace, enter into any Agreement or Compact with another State, or with a foreign Power, or engage in War, unless actually invaded, or in such imminent Danger as will not admit of delay.

Article. II.

Section. 1. The executive Power shall be vested in a President of the United States of America. He shall hold his Office during the Term of four Years, and, together with the Vice President, chosen for the same Term, be elected, as follows

Each State shall appoint, in such Manner as the Legislature thereof may direct, a Number of Electors, equal to the whole Number of Senators and Representatives to which the State may be entitled in the Congress: but no Senator or Representative, or Person holding an Office of Trust or Profit under the United States, shall be appointed an Elector.

The Electors shall meet in their respective States, and vote by Ballot for two Persons, of whom one at least shall not be an Inhabitant of the same State with themselves. And they shall make a List of all the Persons voted for, and of the Number of Votes for each; which List they shall sign and certify, and transmit sealed to the Seat of the Government of the United States, directed to the President of the Senate. The President of the Senate shall, in the Presence of the Senate and House of Representatives, open all the Certificates, and the Votes shall then be counted. The Person having the greatest Number of Votes shall be the President, if such Number be a Majority of the whole Number of Electors appointed; and if there be more than one who have such Majority, and have an equal Number of Votes, then the House of Representatives shall immediately chuse by Ballot one of them for President; and if no Person have a Majority, then from the five highest on the List the said House shall in like Manner chuse the President. But in chusing the President, the Votes shall be taken by States, the Representation from each State having one Vote; A quorum for this Purpose shall consist of a Member or Members from two thirds of the States, and a Majority of all the States shall be necessary to a Choice. In every Case, after the Choice of the President, the Person having the greatest Number of Votes of the Electors shall be the Vice President. But if there should remain two or more who have equal Votes, the Senate shall chuse from them by Ballot the Vice President.

The Congress may determine the Time of chusing the Electors, and the Day on which they shall give their Votes; which Day shall be the same throughout the United States.

No Person except a natural born Citizen, or a Citizen of the United States, at the time of the Adoption of this Constitution, shall be eligible to the Office of President; neither shall any Person be eligible to that Office who shall not have attained to the Age of thirty five Years, and been fourteen Years a Resident within the United States.

In Case of the Removal of the President from Office, or of his Death, Resignation, or Inability to discharge the Powers and Duties of the said Office, the Same shall devolve on the Vice President, and the Congress may by Law provide for the Case of Removal, Death, Resignation or Inability, both of the President and Vice President, declaring what Officer shall then act as President, and such Officer shall act accordingly, until the Disability be removed, or a President shall be elected.

The President shall, at stated Times, receive for his Services, a Compensation, which shall neither be encreased nor diminished during the Period for which he shall have been elected, and he shall not receive within that Period any other Emolument from the United States, or any of them.

Before he enter on the Execution of his Office, he shall take the following Oath or Affirmation: "I do solemnly swear (or affirm) that I will faithfully execute the Office of President of the United States, and will to the best of my Ability, preserve, protect and defend the Constitution of the United States."

Section. 2. The President shall be Commander in Chief of the Army and Navy of the United States, and of the Militia of the several States, when called into the actual Service of the United States; he may require the Opinion, in writing, of the principal Officer in each of the executive Departments, upon any Subject relating to the Duties of their respective Offices, and he shall have Power to grant Reprieves and Pardons for Offences against the United States, except in Cases of Impeachment.

He shall have Power, by and with the Advice and Consent of the Senate, to make Treaties, provided two thirds of the Senators present concur; and he shall nominate, and by and with the Advice and Consent of the Senate, shall appoint Ambassadors, other public Ministers and Consuls, Judges of the supreme Court, and all other Officers of the United States, whose Appointments are not herein otherwise provided for, and which shall be established by Law: but the Congress may by Law vest the Appointment of such inferior Officers, as they think proper, in the President alone, in the Courts of Law, or in the Heads of Departments. The President shall have Power to fill up all Vacancies that may happen during the Recess of the Senate, by granting Commissions which shall expire at the End of their next Session.

Section. 3. He shall from time to time give to the Congress Information of the State of the Union, and recommend to their Consideration such

Measures as he shall judge necessary and expedient; he may, on extraordinary Occasions, convene both Houses, or either of them, and in Case of Disagreement between them, with Respect to the Time of Adjournment, he may adjourn them to such Time as he shall think proper; he shall receive Ambassadors and other public Ministers; he shall take Care that the Laws be faithfully executed, and shall Commission all the Officers of the United States.

Section. 4. The President, Vice President and all civil Officers of the United States, shall be removed from Office on Impeachment for, and Conviction of, Treason, Bribery, or other high Crimes and Misdemeanors.

Article III.

Section. 1. The judicial Power of the United States, shall be vested in one supreme Court, and in such inferior Courts as the Congress may from time to time ordain and establish. The Judges, both of the supreme and inferior Courts, shall hold their Offices during good Behaviour, and shall, at stated Times, receive for their Services, a Compensation, which shall not be diminished during their Continuance in Office.

Section. 2. The judicial Power shall extend to all Cases, in Law and Equity, arising under this Constitution, the Laws of the United States, and Treaties made, or which shall be made, under their Authority;—to all Cases affecting Ambassadors, other public Ministers and Consuls;—to all Cases of admiralty and maritime Jurisdiction;—to Controversies to which the United States shall be a Party;—to Controversies between two or more States;— between a State and Citizens of another State,— between Citizens of different States,—between Citizens of the same State claiming Lands under Grants of different States, and between a State, or the Citizens thereof, and foreign States, Citizens or Subjects.

In all Cases affecting Ambassadors, other public Ministers and Consuls, and those in which a State shall be Party, the supreme Court shall have original Jurisdiction. In all the other Cases before mentioned, the supreme Court shall have appellate Jurisdiction, both as to Law and Fact, with such Exceptions, and under such Regulations as the Congress shall make.

The Trial of all Crimes, except in Cases of Impeachment, shall be by Jury; and such Trial shall be held in the State where the said Crimes shall have been committed; but when not committed within any State, the Trial shall be at such Place or Places as the Congress may by Law have directed.

Section. 3. Treason against the United States, shall consist only in levying War against them, or in adhering to their Enemies, giving them Aid and Comfort. No Person shall be convicted of Treason unless on the Testimony of two Witnesses to the same overt Act, or on Confession in open Court.

The Congress shall have Power to declare the Punishment of Treason, but no Attainder of Treason shall work Corruption of Blood, or Forfeiture except during the Life of the Person attainted.

Article. IV.

Section. 1. Full Faith and Credit shall be given in each State to the public Acts, Records, and judicial Proceedings of every other State. And the Congress may by general Laws prescribe the Manner in which such Acts, Records and Proceedings shall be proved, and the Effect thereof.

Section. 2. The Citizens of each State shall be entitled to all Privileges and Immunities of Citizens in the several States.

A Person charged in any State with Treason, Felony, or other Crime, who shall flee from Justice, and be found in another State, shall on Demand of the executive Authority of the State from which he fled, be delivered up, to be removed to the State having Jurisdiction of the Crime.

No Person held to Service or Labour in one State, under the Laws thereof, escaping into another, shall, in Consequence of any Law or Regulation therein, be discharged from such Service or Labour, but shall be delivered up on Claim of the Party to whom such Service or Labour may be due.

Section. 3. New States may be admitted by the Congress into this Union; but no new State shall be formed or erected within the Jurisdiction of any other State; nor any State be formed by the Junction of two or more States, or Parts of States, without the Consent of the Legislatures of the States concerned as well as of the Congress.

The Congress shall have Power to dispose of and make all needful Rules and Regulations respecting the Territory or other Property belonging to the United States; and nothing in this Constitution shall be so construed as to Prejudice any Claims of the United States, or of any particular State.

Section. 4. The United States shall guarantee to every State in this Union a Republican Form of Government, and shall protect each of them against Invasion; and on Application of the Legislature, or of the Executive (when the Legislature cannot be convened), against domestic Violence.

Article. V.

The Congress, whenever two thirds of both Houses shall deem it necessary, shall propose Amendments to this Constitution, or, on the Application of the Legislatures of two thirds of the several States, shall call a Convention for proposing Amendments, which, in either Case, shall be valid to all Intents and Purposes, as Part of this Constitution, when ratified by the Legislatures of three fourths of the several States, or by Conventions in three fourths thereof, as the one or the other Mode of Ratification may be proposed by the Congress; Provided that no

Amendment which may be made prior to the Year One thousand eight hundred and eight shall in any Manner affect the first and fourth Clauses in the Ninth Section of the first Article; and that no State, without its Consent, shall be deprived of its equal Suffrage in the Senate.

Article. VI.

All Debts contracted and Engagements entered into, before the Adoption of this Constitution, shall be as valid against the United States under this Constitution, as under the Confederation.

This Constitution, and the Laws of the United States which shall be made in Pursuance thereof; and all Treaties made, or which shall be made, under the Authority of the United States, shall be the supreme Law of the Land; and the Judges in every State shall be bound thereby, any Thing in the Constitution or Laws of any State to the Contrary notwithstanding.

The Senators and Representatives before mentioned, and the Members of the several State Legislatures, and all executive and judicial Officers, both of the United States and of the several States, shall be bound by Oath or Affirmation, to support this Constitution; but no religious Test shall ever be required as a Qualification to any Office or public Trust under the United States.

Article. VII.

The Ratification of the Conventions of nine States, shall be sufficient for the Establishment of this Constitution between the States so ratifying the Same.

The Word, "the," being interlined between the seventh and eighth Lines of the first Page, The Word "Thirty" being partly written on an Erazure in the fifteenth Line of the first Page, The Words "is tried" being interlined between the thirty second and thirty third Lines of the first Page and the Word "the" being interlined between the forty third and forty fourth Lines of the second Page.

Attest William Jackson Secretary

done in Convention by the Unanimous Consent of the States present the Seventeenth Day of September in the Year of our Lord one thousand seven hundred and Eighty seven and of the Independance of the United States of America the Twelfth In witness whereof We have hereunto subscribed our Names,

G°. Washington
Presidt and deputy from Virginia
Delaware: Geo: Read, Gunning Bedford jun, John Dickinson, Richard Bassett, Jaco: Broom
Maryland: James McHenry, Dan of St Thos. Jenifer, Danl. Carroll
Virginia: John Blair, James Madison Jr.
North Carolina: Wm. Blount, Richd. Dobbs Spaight, Hu Williamson

South Carolina: J. Rutledge, Charles Cotesworth Pinckney
Charles Pinckney, Pierce Butler
Georgia: William Few, Abr Baldwin
New Hampshire: John Langdon,Nicholas Gilman
Massachusetts: Nathaniel Gorham, Rufus King
Connecticut: Wm. Saml. Johnson, Roger Sherman
New York: Alexander Hamilton
New Jersey: Wil: Livingston, David Brearley, Wm. Paterson, Jona:
Dayton
Pensylvania: B Franklin, Thomas Mifflin, Robt. Morris, Geo. Clymer,
Thos. FitzSimons, Jared Ingersoll, James Wilson, Gouv Morris

Appendix 3
The Bill of Rights

Amendment I
Congress shall make no law respecting an establishment of religion, or prohibiting the free exercise thereof; or abridging the freedom of speech, or of the press; or the right of the people peaceably to assemble, and to petition the Government for a redress of grievances.

Amendment II
A well regulated Militia, being necessary to the security of a free State, the right of the people to keep and bear Arms, shall not be infringed.

Amendment III
No Soldier shall, in time of peace be quartered in any house, without the consent of the Owner, nor in time of war, but in a manner to be prescribed by law.

Amendment IV
The right of the people to be secure in their persons, houses, papers, and effects, against unreasonable searches and seizures, shall not be violated, and no Warrants shall issue, but upon probable cause, supported by Oath or affirmation, and particularly describing the place to be searched, and the persons or things to be seized.

Amendment V
No person shall be held to answer for a capital, or otherwise infamous crime, unless on a presentment or indictment of a Grand Jury, except in cases arising in the land or naval forces, or in the Militia, when in actual service in time of War or public danger; nor shall any person be subject for the same offence to be twice put in jeopardy of life or limb; nor shall be compelled in any criminal case to be a witness against himself, nor be deprived of life, liberty, or property, without due process of law; nor shall private property be taken for public use, without just compensation.

Amendment VI
In all criminal prosecutions, the accused shall enjoy the right to a speedy and public trial, by an impartial jury of the State and district wherein the crime shall have been committed, which district shall have been previously ascertained by law, and to be informed of the nature and cause of the accusation; to be confronted with the witnesses against him; to have compulsory process for obtaining witnesses in his favor, and to have the Assistance of Counsel for his defence.

Amendment VII
In Suits at common law, where the value in controversy shall exceed twenty dollars, the right of trial by jury shall be preserved, and no fact

tried by a jury, shall be otherwise re-examined in any Court of the United States, than according to the rules of the common law.

Amendment VIII

Excessive bail shall not be required, nor excessive fines imposed, nor cruel and unusual punishments inflicted.

Amendment IX

The enumeration in the Constitution, of certain rights, shall not be construed to deny or disparage others retained by the people.

Amendment X

The powers not delegated to the United States by the Constitution, nor prohibited by it to the States, are reserved to the States respectively, or to the people.

About the Author

In a television interview, talk show host Vincent Dacquino introduced Dr. Larry A. Maxwell to the audience as a *Man of Many Hats*. He is a historian, author, husband, father, grandfather, homeowner, pastor, historian, re-enactor, tailor, musician, document examiner, autograph authenticator, consultant, conference speaker and first responder.

He became politically active during High School, where he worked with the campaign to elect Sen. Edmund Muskie as the nominee for President for the Democrat Party and then helped with numerous other campaigns over the years. He attended Liberty University and was involved when his pastor Dr. Jerry Falwell formed *Moral Majority*, a coalition of Christian, Catholic and Jewish leaders along with Family Organizations and Conservative groups.

He was the Founder and President of *Habitat for Humanity of Putnam County,* New York. President of *The Hudson Valley Trust,* which helps promote and protect the agricultural, architectural and historical resource of the Hudson Valley.

He has served a number of years as a member of the *Southern Baptist Disaster Relief Program*, in partnership with the U.S. Department of Homeland Security. He is also a first responder with the Patterson Fire Department.

His writing career started as the literary editor for his award winning high school yearbook. He later became a journalist and photographer for *The Times of Ti, The Glens Falls Post Star* and the *United Press International (UPI). The Associated Press* honored his journalism from among all reporters in the United States with its First Place Writing Award.

You may contact him with questions, or to schedule appearances on radio or television, or to speak at a seminar, workshop or conferences via his website LarryMaxwell.com

Some Other Books
Written by Larry A. Maxwell

Most of these books are available on Amazon.com. Some are available on Kindle.

More Than 500 Proven Ways to Reduce Expenses

More Than 200 Extreme Ways to Reduce Expenses

Gaining Personal Financial Freedom

Now and Then, Putnam County, New York

Unraveling the Holy Spirit Controversy

How to Find the Right Pastor

Index

13th Amendment 51

14th Amendment 52

1910 Election 16

1948 Election 24

1952 Election 25

1960 Election 18, 24

1972 Election 38, 46

1984 Book 35

1984 Election 18

2000 Election 18

2004 Election 8

2008 Election 13, 47, 53

2010 Election 14

2012 Election 7-8, 53

2016 Election 36, 41, 43, 46, 50, 57

Abante, Benny 49

Abolish Slavery ... 48-49, 51

Absentee Ballot ... 13-14, 47-48, 55

ACORN 47

Adams, John ... 19-20, 78, 91

Adams, John Q. 17

Adirondack Mtn. Club . 27-28

Adirondack Rebellion ... 28-29, 48

Administrative Positions ... 72-73

African American 52

Ailes, Roger 43

Alexander, De Alva 16

Am. Presidency Project 8

Amiri, Shahram 37

Apostle Paul 40

Armstrong, Neil 25

Arrogance 36-38

Assange, Julian 51

Assassination ... 25-26, 48-50

Associated Press 29

Associates 45, 66

Assn. of Comm. Org. 47

Ban on Christians 40

Ban on Muslims 40

Beck, Glenn 30-31

Benevolence 51

Benghazi, Libya 32

Bias 24,26, 29-32

Big Brother 35-36

Black Panthers 52

Brinkley, David 25

Branches of Govt. 67-71

Brooks, Preston 48

Bush, George W. 8, 17-18, 53

Buy Influence 43-43

China 19

Christian Nation ... 19-22, 32

Christian Principles 20-22

Church of Holy Trinity ... 21

Clinton, Bill 51

Clinton, Hillary 33, 37-38, 40, 41, 43, 50-51, 57-58

Clinton, Foundation 38
Coercion 51-52
Commander-in-Chief .. 70, 85
Community Service 65
Congress 22, 50, 52, 54, 67-68, 73, 75, 79-87, 90
Congressional Record 66
Connally, John 49
Constitution 17-20, 22, 53-56, 52-64, 70-71, 79-89
Cooping 9
Corcoran, Jimmy 52
Cruz, Ted 42
Cuomo, Mario 27-29, 48
Danbury Baptist Assn. 53
Dead Vote 9, 47
Declaration of Independence 20-21, 75-78
Democracy 17-19
Democrat ... 16, 16, 18, 24-25, 36-41, 43, 46, 48, 53-53
Democratic Party ... 7, 35-36, 38-39, 50-52, 57
Democratic Repub. ... 18-19
Dewey, Thomas 24
Disinformation 33
Duties 72-73
E-mail 37, 50-51
Earth First! 27-29
Education ... 34, 36, 58, 60, 62, 72
Eisenhower, Dwight 24
Establishment Clause ... 54, 90

Esty, Elizabeth 57
Executive Branch 69-70
FactCheck.org 31
Fair Share 42
False Accusations 39-42
Farrakhan, Louis Sr. 30
Falwell, Jerry 23
Flat Tax 42
Fluid Document 63-64
Forging Signatures 46
Form of Government ... 17-22
Founding Fathers 20-23, 55, 61, 63-64, 67
Fox News 24, 43
Free Exercise Clause 54-55, 90
Gandhi, Indira 49
Gandhi, Rajiv 49
Glenn, John 25
Gore, Al 17, 53
Greater Good 26
Hamilton, Alexander ... 63, 89
Harrison, Benjamin 17
Hayes, Rutherford B. ...., 17
Humanistic 61-62
Huntley, Chet 25
Income Tax 42
Independent Party 12-13
India 19, 29, 49
Internet Search 65
Invalid Registrations 47
Irish 52
Jefferson, Thomas 20, 54, 64, 78

Jim Crow Laws 52

Johnson, Harry 15

Jobs 26, 38, 40, 43, 46, 58, 59, 64-65, 71-72

Judaism 22

Judicial Branch ... 70-71, 86-88

Keitt, Laurence 49

Kennedy, John F. 18, 25, 49-50

Kennedy, Robert 25, 50

King, Martin Luther ... 26, 50

Ku Klux Klan (KKK) .. 50, 52

Legislative Branch 67-71

Letterman, David 53

Liberty University 35

Lies ... 26, 29, 32-34, 40, 42

Lincoln, Abraham 51

Lobbyists 43-44

Malcom X 50

Manipulation ... 26, 31, 33, 42

Maxwell, Herbert 24-26

Maxwell, John H. 52-53

Maxwell, Matt 57-60

McCain, John 13

McGovern, George 38-39

Means, Russell 35

Media ... 10, 22-32, 34, 39-40

Military Ballots 14

Military Reconstruction Act ... 52

Military Weapons 63-64

Million Man March 30

Mobsters 43

Moral Absolutism 60-61

Morton, Marcus 16

Multiple Registrations 46-47

Murphy, Austin 46

Muskie, Edmund 38-39

Muslim, Barbary Pirates ... 19-20

Mysterious Death ... 48, 50-51

NBC 24-25

Native American 35, 52

New York Senator 33-34, 46, 66

Nixon, Richard M. 18, 38-39

Non-Administrative Positions ... 72-73

Nursing Home Votes 40

Obama, Barack Hussein ... 7-8, 13-14, 33, 37, 40, 47, 53

Oligarchy 19, 22

One Vote 15-16, 32, 45

Original Intent 28, 63-64

Orwell, George 35

PAC 44

Party, Joining 12-13

Paul, Rand 41

Personal Attacks 41

Philadelphia 53

Philosophy .. 53, 61-62, 70-71

Photo Id. 45-46, 61

Platform 36, 51, 58-61

Poe, Edgar Allen 8

Political Action Committee ... 42

Political Ads 41-42, 44

Political Correctness ... 34-36

Political favors 38, 43, 57, 68

Political Party 7-9, 12-13, 16, 34, 36, 41, 46, 50-52, 57-59

Position Papers 58-59

Power Brokers 43-44, 74

Power Corrupts 44-45

Pro-Slavery 48-49, 51

Qualifications 23, 72-73, 79-80, 88

Ramos, Fidel 50

Reconstruction 50, 52

Reagan, Ronald 18

Register to Vote ... 11-13, 45-47

Relativism 62

Republic 15, 17-19

Republican 7, 13, 18, 24-25, 32, 33, 39-41, 50, 53

Republican Party 7, 37, 40, 51-52

Restore Honor Rally 30

Revolutionary War ... 15, 54, 64

Rich, Seth 51

Russian Federation 19

Romney, Mitt 7-8

Rule of Law 17, 19, 56

Sanders, Bernie 50, 58

School Board 11-12, 58

School Budget 12

Second Amendment ... 63-64, 90

Senate 15, 22, 48-49, 51, 66-68, 70, 79-82, 84-85, 88

Separation of Church & State ... 53-55

Sharpton, Al 31

Sincerity 23-24

Situational Ethics 61-62

Skills 69, 72-73

Slaves 48-49, 51-52, 63

Smith, Charles 16

Snopes.com 31-32

Soros, George 43

South Korea 18

Specific Issues 58-61

Stewart, Charles III 13

Stones of Shame 28

Sumner, Charles 48-49

Super Delegates 57

Supreme Court 63, 70-71, 82, 85-86

Syrian Christians 40

Tammany Hall 52-53

Teletype Machines 25

Texas 15, 32, 49

The Glens Falls Post Star ... 26, 29

The Times of Ti 27

Thumper 41

Track Record 64-66

Treaty of Paris 21

Treaty of Tripoli 19-20
Truman, Harry 24
Trump, Donald 40-41, 50
Unions 44, 52-53
United Nations 27, 60
United Press (UPI) 29
Using Other Names 47
Vote early, vote often 45
Voter Fraud 8-9, 45-48
Voter Guides 59-60, 66
War Between the States ...
50-52
Watergate 38-39
WikiLeaks 51
Wisdom 74

Before You Vote